Understanding Christianity

*17 Lessons of Christian Essentials for Those
Examining or Embracing the Faith.*

William Frye

Complements the workbook Understanding the Faith by Stephen Smallman, 2009. See introduction.

Scriptures in New International Version.
All annotations to scripture including underline, bold, parenthesis, and italic are by the author for emphasis.

Westminster Catechisms in both traditional language and modern English.

To My Students

Most recently Caleb, Eva, Maggie, and Victor
who inspired me to turn our lessons into this book.

Eva —

I am so grateful
for you!.

Mr. Frye

SEPT 2015

The Seventeen Lessons

Introduction

One of the great joys in my life has been to teach young adults the fundamentals of the Christian faith. These "fundamentals" are not simply the foundation of one religion called Christianity, but properly understood are the essential basis of all truth and human purpose. I have always shared with students in the first lesson of a communicant's class that the first question and answer of the Westminster Shorter Catechism should be the essence and summary passion of their entire life.

Q. What is the chief end of man?

A. The Chief End of Man is to Glorify God and Enjoy him forever.

All of life is illuminated, informed, directed, and inspired by what God has wonderfully appointed as our purpose. For all those in Christ it is a life and purpose that will never end.

One age group that I love to teach is Middle School. These young adults are at the pivotal time of life that combines wonder and openness with a growing intellect and maturity. It is a golden window of time for establishing the Christian mind and heart. This time we used Stephen Smallman's excellent workbook - *Understanding the Faith*. I wrote lessons around each chapter in the book that explored a combination of questions and answers along with scripture reading, stories, examples, prayer, and catechism question memorization. It would be hard to express how much I was blessed to be part of their lives and explore Christianity together.

The book you are holding is a collection of those 17 lessons. During the class I provided the written lesson to both student and parents after each session. I wanted to create occasions outside of class for reflection and discussion. Within the class we prioritized open discussion as the vehicle for learning. Each meeting was very interactive and participative, which I think we all found to be much more engaging and effective for learning than a traditional classroom where the teacher does the talking and the students take notes. We took the time needed for exploration. In fact, sometimes a single lesson (such as effectual calling) would grow and consume a number of meetings. We started to call the hard but rewarding topics: "Deep Water" discussions. Our minds grew together, and our hearts were inflamed with love for the Gospel and the glorious amazing work of our Savior.

Similarly, in this book, the topic of each lesson is propelled forward through a series of questions and answers. Scriptures, catechism questions, stories, summaries, and prayers fill out the material. My goal is to capture in book form the dynamics of exploration. Accordingly, this book is formatted to facilitate quick recognition of lesson components:

- ***italic bold font for questions***
- *italic normal font for example answers*
- normal font for discussion
- **bold font for statements / stories**
- light gray hatched shading for scripture references, NIV and for table summary points
- Medium gray shading for *catechism questions* and *answers*.

I want to thank Stephen Smallman who encouraged me to publish this work as a further help to teachers and students who desire to understand the Christian faith. Thanks also to Darlene Frye and Norma Bennett for their editing and suggestions.

William (Will) Frye

Grass Valley, California
June 2015

Lesson 1

Our Purpose as People

Created for Joy and Glory

Introduction

Who are you? It is an easy question to understand. But a remarkably hard question to answer. Think about it. Try asking someone. They will probably answer the who question with a "what" answer: what their name is, what city they live in, what city they grew up in, what school they attend or company they work for. But "Who are you?" probes much deeper than our what and where answers. It drives us to address our essence and our purpose. Who are you? Do you as a human being have an essential purpose?

The Purpose of Human Life

If you were to ask one or two of your non-Christian friends what they thought was the purpose of living, what would they say?

> *Most would probably say something like being happy, healthy, wealthy, feeling loved, etc...*

WSC 1. What does the Bible say is Man's Purpose?

> *"To glorify God and enjoy him forever."*

What does this mean to you?

> *That he knows me better than I know myself. That I am made to live for him and that my greatest joy will come when I do that.*

Why We Glorify and Enjoy God	Summary
Genesis 1:27 So God created man in his own image, in the image of God he created him; male and female he created them.	We are made in God's Image.
Romans 11:36 For from him and through him and to him are all things. To him be the glory forever! Amen.	All things exist for God and should glorify him.
Revelation 4:11 You are worthy, our Lord and God, to receive glory and honor and power, for you created all things, and by your will they were created and have their being.	God alone is worthy of our worship.
Psalm 19:1-4 The heavens declare the glory of God; the skies proclaim the work of his hands. 2 Day after day they pour forth speech; night after night they display knowledge. 3 There is no speech or language where their voice is not heard. 4 Their voice goes out into all the earth, their words to the ends of the world.	Creation declares that God is to be praised.
Matthew 22:36-40 Teacher, which is the greatest commandment in the Law?" 37 Jesus replied: "'Love the Lord your God with all your heart and with all your soul and with all your mind.' 38 This is the first and greatest commandment. 39 And the second is like it: 'Love your neighbor as yourself.' 40 All the Law and the Prophets hang on these two commandments.	The greatest commandment is to love God with all that we are.

Matthew 6:28-34	
"And why do you worry about clothes? See how the lilies of the field grow. They do not labor or spin. 29 Yet I tell you that not even Solomon in all his splendor was dressed like one of these. 30 If that is how God clothes the grass of the field, which is here today and tomorrow is thrown into the fire, will he not much more clothe you, O you of little faith? 31 So do not worry, saying, 'What shall we eat?' or 'What shall we drink?' or 'What shall we wear?' 32 For the pagans run after all these things, and your heavenly Father knows that you need them. 33 But seek first his kingdom and his righteousness, and all these things will be given to you as well. 34 Therefore do not worry about tomorrow, for tomorrow will worry about itself. Each day has enough trouble of its own.	God is in control of our lives and we need not worry.
Psalm 73:24-28	
You guide me with your counsel, and afterward you will take me into glory. 25 Whom have I in heaven but you? And earth has nothing I desire besides you. 26 My flesh and my heart may fail, but God is the strength of my heart and my portion forever. 27 Those who are far from you will perish; you destroy all who are unfaithful to you. 28 But as for me, it is good to be near God. I have made the Sovereign LORD my refuge; I will tell of all your deeds.	We are created to desire God and be satisfied by him.

John 17:24	
Father, I want those you have given me to be with me where I am, and to see my glory, the glory you have given me because you loved me before the creation of the world.	Our destiny is to be with God and enjoy his Glory.

How do we Glorify God?

What does it mean to glorify something?

> *To speak well of it, to praise it, put it first, cause other people to think well of it, to bring it honor or recognition.*

What are some things people glorify?

> *Good looks, intelligence, power, leadership, talent.*

What should we glorify most of all?

> *God, as we have learned.*

How do we do that?

How We are to Glorify God	Summary
Psalm 50:23 He who sacrifices thank offerings honors me, and he prepares the way so that I may show him the salvation of God.	Give thanks.
Psalm 86:12 I will praise you, O Lord my God, with all my heart; I will glorify your name forever.	Praise him with our whole heart.
John 4:22-23 Yet a time is coming and has now come when the true worshipers will worship the Father in spirit and truth, for they are the kind of worshipers the Father seeks.	Worship according to God's Word and Spirit.

Matthew 5:15-16 Neither do people light a lamp and put it under a bowl. Instead they put it on its stand, and it gives light to everyone in the house. 16 In the same way, <u>let your light shine before men, that they may see your good deeds and praise your Father in heaven.</u>	Do good deeds.
1 Corinthians 10:31 So whether you eat or drink or whatever you do, do it all for the glory of God.	Do everything to God's glory.
1 Peter 2:12 <u>Live such good lives among the pagans</u> that, though they accuse you of doing wrong, they may see your good deeds and glorify God on the day he visits us.	Live good lives.
Romans 15:5-6 May the God who gives endurance and encouragement give you a spirit of unity among yourselves as you follow Christ Jesus, 6 so that <u>with one heart and mouth you may glorify the God</u> and Father of our Lord Jesus Christ.	Glorify God in unity with others.

Augustine's Quote

In the 5th century A.D. St. Augustine said something very profound:

> "Thou hast made us for thyself and our hearts are restless until they find their rest in thee."

Why are our hearts restless unless resting in God?

We are made to glorify and enjoy God. When we don't we are unfulfilled – something is missing.

What does it mean to enjoy something?

To take pleasure in it, to be satisfied with it, to feel benefit from it.

What are some things people enjoy?

Good food, entertainment, movies, friends, vacations.

What should we enjoy most of all?

God, as we have learned.

How are we to enjoy God?

How We are to Enjoy God	Summary
Psalm 16:8-9 I have set the LORD always before me. Because he is at my right hand, I will not be shaken. 9 Therefore my heart is glad and my tongue rejoices; my body also will rest secure.	True joy comes from the presence of God.
Jeremiah 9:23-24 This is what the LORD says: "Let not the wise man boast of his wisdom or the strong man boast of his strength or the rich man boast of his riches, 24 but let him who boasts boast about this: that he understands and knows me, that I am the LORD, who exercises kindness, justice and righteousness on earth, for in these I delight," declares the LORD.	We delight in knowing who God is and that he delights in justice and righteousness.

Romans 5:8-11 But God demonstrates his own love for us in this: While we were still sinners, Christ died for us. 5:9 Since we have now been justified by his blood, how much more shall we be saved from God's wrath through him! 10 For if, when we were God's enemies, we were reconciled to him through the death of his Son, how much more, having been reconciled, shall we be saved through his life! 11 Not only is this so, but we also rejoice in God through our Lord Jesus Christ, through whom we have now received reconciliation.	We rejoice knowing that we are adopted by God because of the work of Christ.
Psalm 19:7-11 7 The law of the LORD is perfect, reviving the soul. The statutes of the LORD are trustworthy, making wise the simple.8 The precepts of the LORD are right, giving joy to the heart. The commands of the LORD are radiant, giving light to the eyes. 9 The fear of the LORD is pure, enduring forever.The ordinances of the LORD are sure and altogether righteous. 10 They are more precious than gold, than much pure gold; they are sweeter than honey, than honey from the comb. 11 By them is your servant warned; in keeping them there is great reward.	We delight in knowing and keeping God's commands.

Galatians 5:22-23 But the fruit of the Spirit is love, joy, peace, patience, kindness, goodness, faithfulness, 23 gentleness and self-control. Against such things there is no law.	The Holy Spirit produces Joy in our lives.
James 1:2-4 Consider it pure joy, my brothers, whenever you face trials of many kinds, 3 because you know that the testing of your faith develops perseverance. 4 Perseverance must finish its work so that you may be mature and complete, not lacking anything.	We can have joy in suffering in trials because God uses them to mature us.
1 Thessalonians 4:16-18 For the Lord himself will come down from heaven, with a loud command, with the voice of the archangel and with the trumpet call of God, and the dead in Christ will rise first. 17 After that, we who are still alive and are left will be caught up together with them in the clouds to meet the Lord in the air. And so we will be with the Lord forever. 18 Therefore encourage each other with these words.	We have joy that we know that we will be with God forever.

Sin

What is man's choice to disobey God and live without him called?

Sin.

WSC 14. What is sin?

Sin is disobeying or not conforming to God's law in any way.

What are some ways in which we can disobey God?

- Worshipping other gods
- Making idols
- Misusing God's name
- Not keeping the Sabbath
- Not honoring our parents
- Murdering
- Being unfaithful our husband or wife
- Stealing
- Lying
- Longing to have what belongs to another person.

The Greatest Commandment	Summary
Matthew 22:36-37 "Teacher, which is the greatest commandment in the Law?" 37 Jesus replied: "Love the Lord your God with all your heart and with all your soul and with all your mind."	It is sin not to love God with all that we are.

How does this change your thoughts about sin?

Most people think of sin as bad behavior or thoughts. Jesus is saying that sin is fundamentally a love problem – not loving God with all that we are. That is what results in sinful behavior.

God's Response to Sin – A Forgiven and Adopted Family

What is God's plan to rescue his creation?

To provide a savior who will rescue a great number of people from sin, and adopt them into God's family.

Would God have been just (right) if He had chosen not to rescue his creation?

   Yes.

Why did he do it?

   For his pleasure.

Chosen by his Pleasure	Summary
Ephesians 1:4-6 For he chose us in him before the creation of the world to be holy and blameless in his sight. In love 5 he predestined us to be adopted as his sons through Jesus Christ, in accordance with his pleasure and will – 6 to the praise of his glorious grace, which he has freely given us in the One he loves.	Before the world was created God chose us to his holy children.

The Church

What is this family called?

   The Church (called out ones)

   The Body of Christ

The Sacraments

The church has a responsibility to administer the ordinances that Christ appointed to benefit his church.

WSC 92. What is a sacrament?

A sacrament is a holy ordinance appointed by Christ, by which, by visible signs, Christ, and the benefits of the new covenant, are represented, sealed and applied to believers.

WSC 93. What are the sacraments of the New Testament?

The sacraments of the New Testament are Baptism and the Lord's Supper, and these take the place of Circumcision and the Passover in the Old Testament.

Who established these sacraments?

Jesus.

Matthew 28:19

Therefore go and make disciples of all nations, baptizing them in the name of the Father and of the Son and of the Holy Spirit.

1 Corinthians 11:23-26

For I received from the Lord what I also passed on to you: The Lord Jesus, on the night he was betrayed, took bread, 24 and when he had given thanks, he broke it and said, "This is my body, which is for you; do this in remembrance of me." 25 In the same way, after supper he took the cup, saying, "This cup is the new covenant in my blood; do this, whenever you drink it, in remembrance of me." 26 For whenever you eat this bread and drink this cup, you proclaim the Lord's death until he comes.

Who should be baptized?

Anyone, who confesses Jesus Christ, as Savior and Lord should be baptized.

Note – some churches also baptize young children of parents who are confessing Christians. In this case, baptism is not thought of as something that itself secures salvation for the child, but rather is recognition that the child is a member of the church (a parallel to child circumcision in the Old Testament). If the baptized child subsequently makes a confession of Christ, they are then admitted to the Lord's Supper. For more see WSC 95.

How is one able to receive the Lord's Supper?

By confessing Jesus Christ, as Savior and Lord, and usually following baptism.

Who are you? What is your purpose?

"To glorify God and enjoy him forever" (WSC 1)

It is <u>the</u> answer to build your life around and upon.

<u>Review</u>

Lesson 1 – We as people have a purpose from God: To glorify him and enjoy him forever. This purpose brings meaning and direction for all of our life.

Prayer

- Father – we ask you to help us to see your glory more clearly
  - That we would see your glory in your creation
  - That we would see your glory in your Word
  - That we would see your glory in how you have provided salvation for your people
  - That we would live to glorify and Enjoy you above all else
  - That we would give thanks continually
  - That we would live obedient lives
  - That we would love our neighbor
  - That we would worship you with other believers
- Father – prepare us to confess you as Savior if we have not yet done so; we want to know our true and God given purpose

Lesson 2

How God Can Be Known

The Scriptures and Creation

Introduction

Your purpose is to glorify and enjoy God. But how do you do that? Where do you begin? Of course, it must begin with knowing who God is and what it means to bring him glory and enjoy him. How do we get this knowledge? Certainly, our world abounds with different ideas about God. Many religions and philosophies (including atheism which denies God completely) assert different and contradicting claims. But which is true? Are any true? How can we be sure?

Revelation – How do we learn about God?

What are some ideas that people have about God?

- *Some think he doesn't even exist – he is a fairy tale.*

- *Some think God exists but does not involve himself in the world.*

- *Some think everything that exists is God.*

- *Some think he may exist but is very limited in power and can't control evil.*

What are some ideas people have about how the universe began?

- *Some think that the universe has always been here forever and that it was not created.*

- *Some think that the universe came out of nothing at the time of the Big Bang.*

- *Some think that all of life came about by chance over a very long time through the process of evolution.*

What does the word "revelation" mean?

Revelation means disclosing or revealing that which was previously hidden; what was not perceivable becomes perceivable.

How many ways can you think of that people have learned about God?

- *Observing creation, and thinking that it was created.*

- *Some (a few) have heard a true prophet speak directly to them (e.g. the OT prophets, Christ).*

- *Most people have read God's Word as it has been written down – the words of the prophets and apostles – the Bible.*

How does God reveal himself in creation?

Creation tells us that God is great, mighty, powerful, and intelligent. We see design all around us.

> **Romans 1:20**
> For since the creation of the world God's invisible qualities -- his eternal power and divine nature – have been clearly seen being understood by what has been made, so that men are without excuse.

Someone says "I never had a chance to read the Bible, so there is no way God can hold me responsible for not believing that he exists". What do you think?

Romans 1 says that is not a good excuse, because what God has made speaks of his existence and his power.

> **Psalm 19:1**
>
> The heavens declare the glory of God; the skies proclaim the work of his hands.

So, how can one be an atheist if creation speaks so clearly? Is this an intelligence problem? What is going on?

> **Romans 1:18-19**
>
> The wrath of God is being revealed from heaven against all the godlessness and wickedness of men who suppress the truth by their wickedness, 19 since what may be known about God is plain to them, because God has made it plain to them.

This is a result of the fall of man – in our sin we deny what God reveals. In fact we hold it down (suppress). Returning to the example of the curtain, it is like the curtain is pulled back revealing the truth, but we move the curtain to cover it up again. But sadly we do more; we hold the curtain in place to hide the truth as it struggles to come out.

It is as if sin puts a blanket over our minds. We are in the dark and prefer it that way.

> **John 1:3-5**
>
> Through him all things were made; without him nothing was made that has been made. In him was life, and that life was the light of men. The light shines in the darkness, but the darkness has not understood it

How else does God hold us accountable?

Romans 2 says that if you do by nature what God requires then it becomes the law (standard) that is written on your heart. God will then judge you based upon that law.

If your conscience never bothers you, it merely shows your sinfulness.

> **Romans 2:14-16**
>
> Indeed, when Gentiles, who do not have the law, do by nature things required by the law, they are a law for themselves, even though they do not have the law, 15 since they show that the requirements of the law are written on their hearts, their consciences also bearing witness, and their thoughts now accusing, now even defending them. 16 This will take place on the day when God will judge men's secrets through Jesus Christ, as my gospel declares.

Even if we have never heard God's commands, we might naturally try to do many of the things the law of God requires. When we do this we show we have accepted the law as a standard. When we fail to obey that law we feel accused by our conscience. God will one day judge us by that law that is written on our heart.

Is your conscience reliable guide for our conduct?

No. The conscience merely tells us if we are living according to our own beliefs. Those beliefs can be very wrong. Our consciences can lead us to do things that don't honor God.

Consider this story:

My name is Charlie. I am a young boy growing up on a remote island. I have been on this island for as long as I can remember. All that my brother and I have is what the island has provided. This island has beautiful sandy beaches, plenty of fish and fruit to eat, and perfect weather. When I look at the beauty of the island and its plant and wild life I have become convinced that it is like a piece of art and that there must be an artist. Everything is wonderfully complex and works together in ways that are amazing. I know that I make things. I have used my intelligence and skills to build a hut for shelter, fishing poles and spears to catch food, and a bed woven of banana leaves. I am quite proud of these creations. But when compared to the Island, they seem simple, to say the least. I realize that whoever made this island is incredibly more intelligent and powerful and creative than I am. I don't have a good name for this creator, but I have started to use the name "Master Creator" when I think and talk about him.

Yesterday I was very hungry and decided to take a coconut from my brother's food pile. I did this even though I had plenty of food in my own stack. Later that day I was feeling really bad that I had taken the coconut without asking. I know I wouldn't like it if my brother did that with my coconuts. I thought about the island and the Master Creator and it came to me that he must have also made and might disapprove of what I did. If he is my creator he would probably have the right to require that I live in a certain way. Maybe these guilty feelings are from him, to show me that he is offended. Today, I continue to be worried that he may be angry with me. I feel unsettled and anxious. What should I do?

What do you think Charlie will do?

He might try giving one of his coconuts to his brother as a replacement. He might also do nothing and wait and see if his anxiety lessens.

Back to the story:

I think I will try to make nice with the Master Creator, just in case he is angry with me. I gather some coconuts, make a fire, and cook some coconuts. I leave them on the big rock by the shore. I am not sure this will please the Master Creator, but it is possible he will appreciate the gesture. Just as I am feeling better a storm comes in and destroys my hut. I think that this must be Master Creator punishing me. I make another fire and burn some more coconut offerings. I am now convinced that he is angry with me. Is the storm only the beginning? Life is not good.

Sure enough, another storm comes the next morning. My new hut falls down. I now know that the coconut offerings are not enough! Maybe the problem is that I am offending Master Creator by eating coconuts to begin with. Or maybe they are not pleasing to present to him. I need to do something new. I cook some bananas instead and present them.

The storms stop. That is good. Banana offerings seem to work. I am really relieved. I also thought I should replace the coconut I took from my brother. I am still considering if I should warn him about eating coconuts.

It is one week later. I am a little tired of bananas. In fact I have a huge craving for a coconut. The craving grows. I decide to go ahead and dig in to a big juicy coconut. Yum! Tastes so good. Suddenly I feel anxious.

In this story is Charlie developing a reliable understanding of how to be right with Master Creator?

No. Even though Charlie sees in creation that Master Creator (God) exists and is powerful, he has no certain idea how to please him and relieve his conscience. In fact, even though his conscience was aligned with God's commands when it came to stealing, it also accused you of eating coconuts, and God's law says nothing about eating coconuts.

But then Charlie ate a coconut when he thought it is displeasing to God. He feels guilty for disobeying his conscience.

This is a mess!

How can Charlie glorify and enjoy God in this situation?

The best he can do is to obey his conscience. But he doubts his conscience because he is speculating about what Master Creator wants.

What does Charlie need?

He needs God to tell him how to live and how to worship him. He also needs to know how to be reconciled to God and delivered from God's anger and judgment. He needs to hear God speak.

How is that going to happen?

God must again reveal himself. He must speak to Charlie. There is no path of salvation through either creation or conscience. If we are to be right with God then he will have to tell us how.

How does God reliably tell us how to glorify and enjoy him?

WSC 2. What authority from God directs us how to glorify and enjoy him?

The only authority for glorifying and enjoying him is the Bible, which is the Word of God and is made up of the Old and New Testaments.

Okay. We need to hear from God to tell us specifically and clearly how to glorify him.

So how can we know that the Bible is the Word of God?

WLC 4. How does it appear that the Scriptures are of the Word of God?

The Scriptures manifest themselves to be the Word of God, by their majesty and purity; by the consent of all the parts, and the scope of the whole, which is to give all glory to God; by their light and power to convince and convert sinners, to comfort and build up believers unto salvation but the Spirit of God bearing witness by and with the Scriptures in the heart of man, is alone able fully to persuade it that they are the very Word of God.

The Scriptures are Majestic

Hosea 8:12

I have written to him the great things of my law, but they were counted as a strange thing.

1 Corinthians 2:6-7, 13

6 We do, however, speak a message of wisdom among the mature, but not the wisdom of this age or of the rulers of this age, who are coming to nothing. 7 No, we declare God's wisdom, a mystery that has been hidden and that God destined for our glory before time began. 13 This is what we speak, not in words taught us by human wisdom but in words taught by the Spirit, explaining spiritual realities with Spirit-taught words.

Psalm 119:18, 129

Open my eyes that I may see wonderful things in your law.... Your statutes are wonderful; therefore I obey them.

The Scriptures are Pure

Psalm 12:6

The words of the LORD are pure words: as silver tried in a furnace of earth, purified seven times.

Psalm 119:140

Your promises have been thoroughly tested, and your servant loves them.

The Scriptures are Consistent

Acts 10:43

All the prophets testify about him that everyone who believes in him receives forgiveness of sins through his name.

Acts 26:22

But God has helped me to this very day; so I stand here and testify to small and great alike. I am saying nothing beyond what the prophets and Moses said would happen.

The Scriptures Glorify God

Romans 3:19, 27

Now we know that whatever the law says, it says to those who are under the law, so that every mouth may be silenced and the whole world held accountable to God.... Where, then, is boasting? It is excluded. Because of what law? The law that requires works? No, because of the law that requires faith.

The Scriptures Proclaim Truth and Wisdom

Acts 18:28

For he vigorously refuted his Jewish opponents in public debate, proving from the Scriptures that Jesus was the Messiah.

Hebrews 4:12

For the Word of God is alive and active. Sharper than any double-edged sword, it penetrates even to dividing soul and spirit, joints and marrow; it judges the thoughts and attitudes of the heart.

James 1:18

He chose to give us birth through the word of truth, that we might be a kind of firstfruits of all he created.

Psalm 19:7-9

The law of the Lord is perfect, refreshing the soul. The statutes of the Lord are trustworthy, making wise the simple. The precepts of the Lord are right, giving joy to the heart. The commands of the Lord are radiant, giving light to the eyes. The fear of the Lord is pure, enduring forever. The decrees of the Lord are firm, and all of them are righteous.

Romans 15:4

For everything that was written in the past was written to teach us, so that through the endurance taught in the Scriptures and the encouragement they provide we might have hope.

Acts 20:32

Now I commit you to God and to the word of his grace, which can build you up and give you an inheritance among all those who are sanctified.

The Spirit of God Confirms God's Word

John 16:13-14.

13 But when he, the Spirit of truth, comes, he will guide you into all the truth. He will not speak on his own; he will speak only what he hears, and he will tell you what is yet to come. 14 He will glorify me because it is from me that he will receive what he will make known to you.

1 John 2:20, 27

20 But you have an anointing from the Holy One, and all of you know the truth. 27 As for you, the anointing you received from him remains in you, and you do not need anyone to teach you. But as his anointing teaches you about all things and as that anointing is real, not counterfeit—just as it has taught you, remain in him.

John 20:31

But these are *written that you may believe* that Jesus is the Messiah, the Son of God, and that by believing you may have life in his name.

The Bible is the Word of God. So what does the Bible primarily teach us?

WSC 3. What does the Bible primarily teach?

The Bible primarily teaches what man is to believe about God and what God requires about man.

Back to the desert Island story. What understanding would the Bible bring to Charlie's situation?

- God is the creator of all things. He is the Master Creator. The same testimony as Natural Revelation.

- You are to love your brother as yourself.

- Stealing is a violation of God's command. In stealing you sinned against God as well as your brother.

- The answer for your sin is not diet or coconut offerings, but the forgiveness that God himself provides through Jesus.

- You are commanded to repent of your sin and turn to the work of Christ for forgiveness.

- God is faithful to both forgive your sins in Christ and also to cleanse you and your conscience.

- Your life has meaning has meaning – your meaning is in glorifying and enjoying God.

- We could go on and on….

How did God write the Bible? Did he write it out and then drop it from the sky?

Paul wrote this in a letter to Timothy:

2 Timothy 3:14-17

But as for you, continue in what you have learned and have become convinced of, because you know those from whom you learned it, 15 and how from infancy you have known the holy Scriptures, which are able to make you wise for salvation through faith in Christ Jesus. 16 All Scripture is God-breathed and is useful for teaching, rebuking, correcting and training in righteousness, 17 so that the man of God may be thoroughly equipped for every good work.

Scripture is God breathed.

What does it mean that scripture is God breathed?

- Its source is God, not man.

- It comes from within God, from who he is.

- When we talk it is our breath that vibrates our vocal cords and forms our words. Our breath is the way we communicate. So Paul is saying that the scriptures are the words of God.

What are the things that scripture is useful for according to this passage?

Uses of Scripture	Explanation
Teaching	Scripture tells us the truth about God and ourselves.
Rebuking	Scripture tells us what is wrong with us.
Correcting	Scripture puts us on the right path to glorify and enjoy God.
Training in Righteousness	Scripture tells us what God requires and what he prohibits.

We know that men wrote the books of the Bible. But if they wrote it, how can we say that God wrote it?

This is mysterious, but God uses the full mind and personality of the writer so that even though they use their own words, yet he so inspires them that the words they speak and write are truly and fully God's words as well. Peter explains this:

---

2 Peter 1:16-21

16 For we did not follow cleverly devised stories when we told you about the coming of our Lord Jesus Christ in power, but we were eyewitnesses of his majesty. 17 He received honor and glory from God the Father when the voice came to him from the Majestic Glory, saying, "This is my Son, whom I love; with him I am well pleased." 18 We ourselves heard this voice that came from heaven when we were with him on the sacred mountain.

19 We also have the prophetic message as something completely reliable, and you will do well to pay attention to it, as to a light shining in a dark place, until the day dawns and the morning star rises in your hearts. 20 Above all, you must understand that no prophecy of Scripture came about by the prophet's own interpretation of things. 21 For prophecy never had its origin in the human will, but prophets, though human, spoke from God as they were carried along by the Holy Spirit.

Men spoke <u>from God</u> "as they were carried along by the Holy Spirit". God used people to write his Scripture. The Holy Spirit used dozens of people over a period of 1500 years to write the 66 books in such a way that they spoke God's words. Yet they used their own language, and phrases, and their own personality is in the writing. God speaks in and through history.

Human Authors of Scripture		
Moses	Joshua	Samuel
Jeremiah	Ezra	Mordecai
David	Solomon	Isaiah
Ezekiel	Daniel	Hosea
Joel	Amos	Obadiah
Jonah	Micah	Nahum
Habakkuk	Zephaniah	Haggai
Zechariah	Malachi	Matthew
Mark	Luke	John
Paul	James	Peter
Jude	A few others in Psalms	Possibly others than Paul for the book of Hebrews

God reveals himself in two ways

1. General revelation – we see what he has done.
2. Special Revelation – we receive what he has said.

General Revelation	Special Revelation
Makes known God's power and divinity	Makes known God's saving grace
Known through nature	Known via supernatural revelation which culminates in the incarnation of Jesus Christ

Continuous	In redemptive history
Supplies man's natural needs	Supplies redemptive knowledge (Acts 10:1-48; 11:13-18)
Mundane, ordinary, "natural"	Supernatural revelation is direct intervention by God
Universal To all people in all places at all times	Progressive and particular To particular people at particular times
Humanity is without excuse	Directs the sinner to salvation
Job 38-40 Psalm 19 Acts 14:15-17; 17:22-31 Romans 1:18-21; 2:14-16	John 1:1, 14, 18; I Timothy 3:16 Hebrews 1:1-3; Matthew 5:17-18 22:29-32; Luke 16:17; 21:33 John 10:35; II Timothy 3:16 II Peter 1:19-21

Review

Lesson 2 – We need to hear from God directly to live out our purpose. We learned that the voice of God that speaks in creation and our consciences is not enough due to our fallen condition. But God has spoken clearly to us! He has done so through the scriptures and his word teaches us what we must believe about God and what he requires of us.

Prayer

- Father – thank you for the revelation of yourself through your creation
    - Thank you that we see your power and glory in what you have made
    - Thank you that creation calls us to worship you
- Father – thank you for the revelation of yourself through the Bible
    - Thank you that it tells us what we are to believe about you
    - Thank you that it tells us what you require of us
    - Thank you that it tells us what you have done to save us
- Father – Thank you that you bring us joy in receiving your revelation and in living for your glory
- Father – we pray that you would bring more people into your family, to love you, glorify you, and to enjoy you

Lesson 3

What is God Like?

Infinite, Eternal, Unchangeable

Introduction

God has revealed himself to us. His glory is revealed by his creation. As we learned in lesson 2, he has also spoken to us directly in words, so that we can understand who He is and who we are created to be. The character and attributes of God are the topic of this lesson.

> **WSC 3. What does the Bible primarily teach?**
>
> *The Bible primarily teaches what man is to believe about God and what God requires about man.*

If you were to try to tell someone what God is like, based upon what the Bible teaches, what would you say?

- God created the heavens and the earth.

- God is all-powerful.

- God is good.

- God is righteous.

- God is everywhere.

- God never changes.

- God is completely honest and trustworthy.

- God is a tri unity: Father, Son, and Holy Spirit.

- God is in total control of his creation.

What does the Catechism teach us about God?

WSC 4. What is God?

God is a spirit, whose being, wisdom, power, holiness, justice, goodness, and truth are infinite, eternal, and unchangeable.

God is a Spirit

What comes to mind when we use the word spirit?

A spirit is like a ghost, it can pass through walls, it can be everywhere, it has no body, you can't touch it, etc.

How a spirit is different than a physical thing.

A Physical Thing	A Spirit
Can be seen	Can't be seen
Has a shape	Has no shape
Has weight	Cannot be weighed
Has a certain size	Has no size
Can be touched and felt	Can't be touched or felt
Is in only one place at a time	Can be in many places at one time

Scriptures that attribute characteristics of a spirit to God

God is a Spirit	Summary
John 1:18 No one has ever seen God, but the one and only Son, who is himself God and is in closest relationship with the Father, has made him known.	No one has seen God.

Colossians 1:15 The Son is the image of the invisible God, the firstborn over all creation.	God is invisible.
I Timothy 6:16 Who alone is immortal and who lives in unapproachable light, whom no one has seen or can see. To him be honor and might forever. Amen.	God is immortal and cannot be seen.
Luke 24:39 Look at my hands and my feet. It is I myself! Touch me and see; a ghost does not have flesh and bones, as you see I have.	A Spirit has no flesh and bones.
John 4:24 God is spirit, and his worshipers must worship in the Spirit and in truth.	We must worship God in spirit as he is a spirit.
1 Timothy 1:17 Now unto the King eternal, immortal, invisible, the only wise God, be honor and glory for ever and ever. Amen.	God is immortal, invisible, and wise.

The second commandment tells us not to make any idols to worship. Why is it important not to make images of God?

Because God is not limited as any physical object is. Any image we make, no matter how beautiful, cannot represent the infinite God who is a spirit.

Exodus 20:4-5

You shall not make for yourself an idol in the form of anything in heaven above or on the earth beneath or in the waters below.

So we now understand from the Bible that God is spirit. Is God just an invisible force (like gravity)?

> *No. God is a person. God has a mind and will. He makes plans and carries them out.*

God is a Person

The Bible tells us that God is a person and not just a force.

God is a Person	Summary
Acts 14:15 Friends, why are you doing this? We too are only human, like you. We are bringing you good news, telling you to turn from these worthless things to the living God, who made the heavens and the earth and the sea and everything in them.	God is living and creative.
Proverbs 15:3 The eyes of the Lord are everywhere, keeping watch on the wicked and the good.	God sees everywhere.
Psalm 55:16-17 As for me, I call to God, and the Lord saves me. Evening, morning and noon I cry out in distress, and he hears my voice.	God hears us and saves us.
Jeremiah 10:10 But the LORD is the true God, he is the living God, and an everlasting king: at his wrath the earth shall tremble, and the nations shall not be able to abide his indignation.	God is the only real god and he is indignant towards rebellion.

Psalm 103:13 As a father has compassion on his children, so the LORD has compassion on those who fear him;	God is compassionate.
John 3:16-17 "For God so loved the world that he gave his one and only Son, that whoever believes in him shall not perish but have eternal life.	God loves and gives.
Luke 18:19 "Why do you call me good?" Jesus answered. "No one is good-except God alone.	God is good.
Philippians 2:27-28 Indeed he was ill, and almost died. But God had mercy on him, and not on him only but also on me, to spare me sorrow upon sorrow.	God is merciful.

Three Adjectives that Describe God

- God is: **Infinite**
  All of his attributes are without limit.

- God is: **Eternal**
  All of his attributes have always existed and always will.

- God is: **Unchangeable**
  All of his attributes are unalterable.

Seven Attributes of God

Being: God exists, but He exists in a completely unique way. God is self-existent. He does not derive his existence from something else.

Exodus 3:14

God said to Moses, "I am who I am. This is what you are to say to the Israelites: 'I am has sent me to you.

Job 11:7-9

Can you fathom the mysteries of God? Can you probe the limits of the Almighty? 8 They are higher than the heavens above—what can you do? They are deeper than the depths below—what can you know? 9 Their measure is longer than the earth and wider than the sea.

What does this mean?

> *It means God must exist and that without his existence, nothing else could exist. We could say that we "borrow" our existence from God.*

Hebrews 1:1-3

In the past God spoke to our forefathers through the prophets at many times and in various ways, 2 but in these last days he has spoken to us by his Son, whom he appointed heir of all things, and through whom he made the universe. 3 The Son is the radiance of God's glory and the exact representation of his being, sustaining all things by his powerful word.

Wisdom: God is wise. He knows all the answers to all questions and he never makes a mistake in what he thinks, decides, or knows.

Romans 16:27

To God only wise, be glory through Jesus Christ for ever. Amen.

Power: Power is the ability to change things or to make them move. God has infinite power to accomplish whatever He desires.

> **Revelation 4:8**
> Each of the four living creatures had six wings and was covered with eyes all around, even under its wings. Day and night they never stop saying: "Holy, holy, holy is the Lord God Almighty, who was, and is, and is to come."

Holiness: God is perfect in all his goodness and righteousness. God is completely worthy of all worship and devotion.

> **Isaiah 6:3**
> **And they were calling to one another: "Holy, holy, holy is the Lord Almighty; the whole earth is full of his glory."**
> **Revelation 15:4**
> Who will not fear you, Lord, and bring glory to your name? For you alone are holy. All nations will come and worship before you, for your righteous acts have been revealed.

Justice: God is always correct in his judgments and always fair and impartial. No one can question him.

> **Deuteronomy 32:4**
> He is the Rock, his works are perfect, and all his ways are just. A faithful God who does no wrong, upright and just is he.

Goodness: God is completely pure and right and beautiful and lovely.

> **Exodus 34:6**
> And he passed in front of Moses, proclaiming, "The Lord, the Lord, the compassionate and gracious God, slow to anger, abounding in love and faithfulness.

Truth: Every word from God is true and sincere and without fault or question.

> **Psalm 19:7-10**
>
> The law of the Lord is perfect, refreshing the soul. The statutes of the Lord are trustworthy, making wise the simple. 8 The precepts of the Lord are right, giving joy to the heart. The commands of the Lord are radiant, giving light to the eyes. 9 The fear of the Lord is pure, enduring forever. The decrees of the Lord are firm, and all of them are righteous. 10 They are more precious than gold, than much pure gold; they are sweeter than honey, than honey from the honeycomb.

Note that each of these seven aspects of the character of God are infinite (beyond measure), eternal (never ending), and unchangeable (without change).

WSC 4. What is God?

God is a spirit, whose being, wisdom, power, holiness, justice, goodness, and truth are infinite, eternal, and unchangeable.

God is Omni

Sometimes to describe God's perfection the prefix "omni" is used. Omni means all or universal. Each of God's attributes is without limit; they are "Omni".

God as Perfect: Omni	Summary
Psalm 139:1-4 You have searched me, Lord, and you know me. 2 You know when I sit and when I rise; you perceive my thoughts from afar. 3 You discern my going out and my lying down; you are familiar with all my ways. 4 Before a word is on my tongue you, Lord, know it completely.	Omniscient. God knows all that can be known. God knows our every thought and knows beforehand what we will say or do.

Psalm 139:7-12 Where can I go from your Spirit? Where can I flee from your presence? 8 If I go up to the heavens, you are there; if I make my bed in the depths, you are there. 9 If I rise on the wings of the dawn, if I settle on the far side of the sea, 10 even there your hand will guide me, your right hand will hold me fast. 11 If I say, "Surely the darkness will hide me and the light become night around me,"12 even the darkness will not be dark to you; the night will shine like the day, for darkness is as light to you.	Omnipresent. God is everywhere. Nothing is hidden from his sight. There is no place we can go to escape from his presence.
Psalm 135:5-7 I know that the LORD is great, that our Lord is greater than all gods. 6 The LORD does whatever pleases him, in the heavens and on the earth, in the seas and all their depths. 7 He makes clouds rise from the ends of the earth; he sends lightning with the rain and brings out the wind from his storehouses.	Omnipotent. God is able to do whatever pleases him; He does all he desires heaven and on earth.

Our Response to God

An important discipline of the Christian life is to meditate (think upon deeply) on the greatness of God and his Word and great works. We savor who God is and what he has done.

Meditating on and praising God
Psalm 96:4 For great is the LORD and most worthy of praise; he is to be feared above all gods.

Psalm 99:2-3

Great is the LORD in Zion; he is exalted over all the nations. 3 Let them praise your great and awesome name – he is holy.

Psalm 145:3

Great is the LORD and most worthy of praise; his greatness no one can fathom.

1 John 3:1

How great is the love the Father has lavished on us, that we should be called children of God! And that is what we are!

Psalm 48:9

Within your temple, O God, we meditate on your unfailing love.

Psalm 77:12

I will meditate on all your works and consider all your mighty deeds.

Psalm 119:148

My eyes stay open through the watches of the night, that I may meditate on your promises.

Psalm 119:97

Oh, how I love your law! I meditate on it all day long.

Psalm 143:5

I remember the days of long ago; I meditate on all your works and consider what your hands have done.

Psalm 119:15-16

I meditate on your precepts and consider your ways. 16 I delight in your decrees; I will not neglect your word.

Joshua 1:7-8
Do not let this Book of the Law depart from your mouth;
meditate on it day and night, so that you may be careful to do
everything written in it. Then you will be prosperous and
successful.

Psalm 119:27
Let me understand the teaching of your precepts; then I will
meditate on your wonders.

Psalm 119:48
I lift up my hands to your commands, which I love, and I
meditate on your decrees.

Remote Island Story Continued

Things seem much better with my brother now. He asked
me for some bananas from my banana stash a week after my
coconut theft. It seems we both have an understanding about
respecting one another's stuff. I know that he is no longer
angry, and I am glad we are not fighting anymore, but I still
feel bad. The beauty of this island continues to remind me
that someone formed it who is amazingly powerful and
creative. I still worry that the creator of the island, whoever
that may be, might still be upset with me. Yes... I know... I
did try to pay him back with coconut and banana sacrifices
and that did seem to work. There have not been big storms.
Oh well. It is a good day for fishing, enough worrying about
angry island designers.

It is the next morning and I am walking on the white sand
beach about a half-mile from my hut (the rebuilt one).
Walking down the beach I see a strange object that is
wedged between two rocks. When I get closer I see that it is
an old wooden box. I pull it off to the side and start to pry
off the lid. When I finally force it open I find some very

interesting things in it. Inside is a white ball with a handprint on it. That will be fun. I think my brother will be jealous. Next I find a 3 by 5 ft piece of net, and I think: "Awesome, this will make a terrific fishing net". I love it – less time fishing and more time relaxing. Lastly, I find a number of books. The first is full of pictures of a variety of things I have seen and many I have never seen (remember that I have spent my entire life on this island). Under each picture are symbols and shapes. When I show it to my brother he recognizes the symbols as representing the names of objects in the pictures. I don't know how he knows this, but he is older than I and remembers experiences that I don't. I use the book over the next month to learn these written words and how they correspond to the pictures. With this learning I begin reading a small book. With the help of my brother I learn to read this book. It is a story about a small dog and her a little girl who owns her. Reading is a new experience for me and I enjoy it, but I quickly get tired of this book. Fortunately there are many other books to examine and attempt to understand. One of them is called White Fang (my brother explains that a fang is a long sharp tooth). This is a story about a dog, in a very cold place that is filled with ice and snow (to be honest my brother and I have no idea what those things are – but he says that he remembers something about water being like this when it gets really cold outside).

Entry - Six months later.

I love reading. I have read more than 10 books. I can now read and understand almost all of the words (thanks to my brother). He has also enjoyed it because the books have brought back many memories that he had forgotten; memories of places before the island when I was a baby and we lived together in a city with our parents. Unfortunately I don't remember my parents and my brother won't talk about what happened to them.

Today, I just started reading another book. This one is very large and has very small printed words. It seems to be a story about an ancient people who lived in the desert. The book has a weird name – "the Bible". In fact, the first part of the book describes how this amazing being called God created the whole world and put the first two people in a garden. To be honest when I read this I started feeling unsettled. Is this just a story or is this true? If it is true than this being (who I have been calling Master Creator) created everything in the sky and sea, including this island. If that is true I feel really lucky that the coconut and banana sacrifices worked to stop the storms. Because someone who can create the whole world (I learned about how big the world is in one of the science books) could really make a mess of my life if they were really mad… storms might just be the start. Ugh! I need to read more. I am a little scared but this is compelling. I always wanted to know more about who created the island (and apparently everything else). I hope this book can tell me more about him. All for now – I will write again in a few days as I learn more.

Consider these questions about the remote island story in light of what we have learned about God in this lesson.

What will Charlie learn about God? What will he learn that confirms what he knew before? What will surprise him? What questions will it raise for him? Will he be more comforted or more worried?

Review

Lesson 3 – God is a Spirit (not limited in space). God is a person and not a force. God in his Being, wisdom, power holiness, justice, goodness, and truth is infinite, eternal, and unchangeable. God is Omni (all) present, powerful, and knowledgeable. God is worthy of high highest praise and adoration and part of our purpose is to continually meditate on the character and works of God.

<u>Prayer</u>

- Father – thank you that you have revealed who you are in the Scriptures.
    - You are a spirit and not limited to one location or restricted to one time
    - You are infinite, eternal, and unchangeable in your being and majestic character
    - You are worthy of our highest praise and worship
- Father – worshipping you is both our highest duty and our greatest privilege
    - Teach us how you have provided the way of forgiveness and reconciliation
    - Teach us to know and worship you as you want to be known and worshipped

Lesson 4

God the Three in One

Distinct Yet One

Introduction

We have seen that God is a spirit and is infinite, eternal, and
unchangeable. But God reveals even more about himself to us.
He reveals that He is one God, but in three persons. Our mind
responds "Nonsense! Three does not equal one!" We learn the
Trinity is not illogical, but a profound and wonderful mystery.

***Before God can teach us that he is three in one, what do we
need to learn?***

We need to learn there is only one God.

Where do we learn this in the Bible?

Deuteronomy 6:4-5

Hear, O Israel: The LORD our God, the LORD is one. 5 Love
the LORD your God with all your heart and with all your soul
and with all your strength.

Exodus 20:1-3

And God spoke all these words: 2 "I am the LORD your God,
who brought you out of Egypt, out of the land of slavery. 3
"You shall have no other gods before me.

Why is this truth significant?

It is a significant truth because the surrounding nations worshiped many gods and had fallen into idolatry, worshiping the creation rather than the true Creator.

What is the difference between these names of God: Lord and LORD?

Lord:
Master, owner, or lord (Adonai in Hebrew)

LORD:
Yahweh or Jehovah, which means, "to be" or "I AM".
God simply is, he exists always and necessarily.

Exodus 3:14 14

God said to Moses, "I AM WHO I AM. This is what you are to say to the Israelites: 'I AM has sent me to you.'"

Where do we see these different names – Lord and LORD?

Psalm 8:1

O LORD, our Lord, how majestic is your name in all the earth!

Psalm 30:8

To you, O LORD, I called; to the Lord I cried for mercy

Psalm 39:7-8

But now, Lord, what do I look for? My hope is in you. 8 Save me from all my transgressions; do not make me the scorn of fools.

Psalm 23:1-3

The LORD is my shepherd; I shall not be in want. 2 He makes me lie down in green pastures, he leads me beside quiet waters, 3 he restores my soul.

Have you heard other names of God based on Jehovah (LORD)?

The following are other names in honor of the LORD in the Old Testament that stem from the basic name of Yahweh:

Jehovah	Meaning
Jehovah -jireh	This name is translated as "The-LORD-Will-Provide," commemorating the provision of the ram in place of Isaac for Abraham's sacrifice (Gen 22:14).
Jehovah -nissi	This name means "The-LORD-Is-My-Banner," in honor of God's defeat of the Amalekites (Ex 17:15).
Jehovah -shalom	This phrase means "The-LORD-Is-Peace," the name Gideon gave the altar which he built in Ophrah (Judg 6:24).
Jehovah-shammah	This phrase expresses the truth that "The-LORD-Is-There," referring to the city which the prophet Ezekiel saw in his vision (Ezek 48:35).
Jehovah -tsebaoth	This name, translated "The-LORD-of-hosts," was used in the days of David and the prophets, witnessing to God the Savior who is surrounded by his hosts of heavenly power (1 Sam 1:3).
Jehovah -elohe	This name means "LORD-God-of-Israel," and it appears in Isaiah, Jeremiah, and the Psalms.

God in Three Persons

As we read scriptures it becomes increasingly clear that although there is only one God, but that God is three persons. So there is one God (unity), but in three (tri) persons. To express this we use the term Trinity which is short for tri-unity. God is Father, Son, and Holy Spirit.

Does the word Trinity appear in the Bible?

No.

Then why do we believe in the Trinity?

Because the Trinity is clearly and consistently taught in Scripture.

Where do we find it clearly stated that Jesus is God?

Jesus is God	Summary
Matthew 1:22-23 All this took place to fulfill what the Lord had said through the prophet: 23 "The virgin will be with child and will give birth to a son, and they will call him Immanuel"–which means, "God with us."	Jesus is called Immanuel, which means, "God with us".
John 10:29-30 My Father, who has given them to me, is greater than all; no one can snatch them out of my Father's hand. 30 I and the Father are one."	Jesus claims to be one with the Father.
John 8:58-59 "I tell you the truth," Jesus answered, "before Abraham was born, I AM!" 59 At this, they picked up stones to stone him, but Jesus hid himself, slipping away from the temple grounds.	Why stone Jesus for this? It was heresy to the Jews. Jesus was claiming to be Yahweh! The great I AM.

Hebrews 1:3	Jesus is fully God
The Son is the radiance of God's glory and the exact representation of his being, sustaining all things by his powerful word.	and shines with the glory of God.
John 1:1-5	Jesus was with God
In the beginning was the Word, and the Word was with God, and the Word was God. 2 He was with God in the beginning. 3 Through him all things were made; without him nothing was made that has been made. 4 In him was life, and that life was the light of men. 5 The light shines in the darkness, but the darkness has not understood it.	from the beginning and was God.

Where do we see that the Holy Spirit is God?

The Holy Spirit is God	Summary
Genesis 1:1-2	The Spirit of God
In the beginning God created the heavens and the earth. 2 The earth was without form and void, and darkness was upon the face of the deep; and the Spirit of God was moving over the face of the waters.	was active as God created the heavens and the earth.
Matthew 28:19	In the New
Therefore go and make disciples of all nations, baptizing them in the name of the Father and of the Son and of the Holy Spirit.	Testament another name for God is revealed; God's name (not names) is "Father, Son, and Holy Spirit".

Acts 5:3-4 Then Peter said, "Ananias, how is it that Satan has so filled your heart that you have lied to the Holy Spirit and have kept for yourself some of the money you received for the land? 4 Didn't it belong to you before it was sold? And after it was sold, wasn't the money at your disposal? What made you think of doing such a thing? You have not lied to men but to God."	Lying to the Holy Spirit is the same as lying to God.
2 Corinthians 3:18 And we, who with unveiled faces all reflect the Lord's glory, are being transformed into his likeness with ever-increasing glory, which comes from the Lord, who is the Spirit.	The Spirit is the Lord.
1 Corinthians 2:10-11 The Spirit searches all things, even the deep things of God. 11 For who among men knows the thoughts of a man except the man's spirit within him? In the same way no one knows the thoughts of God except the Spirit of God.	Just as a man's spirit knows his thoughts, the Holy Spirit knows God's thoughts.

So, how can we have three persons and yet one God?

WSC 6. How many persons are in the one God?

Three persons are in the one God, the Father, the Son, and the Holy Spirit. These three are one God, the same in substance and equal in power and glory.

When the catechism answer says that God is of one substance, what does this mean?

It does not mean that God is made of some physical material. We learned last week that God is a spirit. It means that Father, Son, and Holy Spirit are equally God.

Are the three persons of the Trinity identical?

No. They differ in their personal properties.

> **John 15:26-27**
> When the Counselor comes, whom I will send to you from the
> Father, the Spirit of truth who goes out from the Father, he will
> testify about me. 27 And you also must testify, for you have
> been with me from the beginning.

Why is the doctrine of the Trinity a stumbling block to many people?

Because it is a mystery which human reason cannot explain.

Does the doctrine of the Trinity contradict itself?

*No. There is a difference between a mystery – something
beyond our understanding, and a contradiction – which is
absurd.*

*The doctrine of the Trinity teaches that God is one in one
sense – being of the same essence or substance, yet three in
another sense – being three persons (personalities).*

*It would be a contradiction to say that the persons of the
Trinity were both the same in substance and different in
substance at the same time, or if it were claimed that there
were three persons in the Godhead and also one person in
the Godhead.*

What are some of the illustrations that have been used to help people understand the Trinity?

*Some have used the egg as an illustration of the Trinity
(yolk, white, shell). Another is fire, light, and heat. Another
is water, heat, and steam.*

Are these good illustrations?

*No. Because the trinity is a divine mystery, which has no
parallels in nature, and has not been revealed in nature.*

Physical illustrations of the Trinity fail:

- They make use of physical differences, which cannot represent relationships between persons.

- Some physical examples illustrate the Trinity through an object with parts. For example, the egg is one egg with three parts, but yolk, white, and shell are clearly different substances. But the Trinity is not made up three different essences, but truly one essence – God.

- Some physical examples illustrate the Trinity through materials that have different properties or expressions under different conditions. For example, water exists in three phases: water, ice, and steam. But the Trinity is not three expressions or organizations of the one God, but is three distinct persons that are one God.

Why is the phrase "same in substance" very important as a test of real belief in the Trinity?

Because some religions teach that Jesus is a god, but are not willing to say that He is the same substance as God the Father. Mormons for example teach that Jesus is god (small g) who was created by God (large G). Muslims believe that Jesus was a great prophet; but not God. Judaism likewise rejects Christ as God.

Into what name of God are Christians baptized?

> **Matthew 28:19**
> Therefore go and make disciples of all nations, baptizing them in the name of the Father and of the Son and of the Holy Spirit

Note that this command does not say "names of the Father and of the Son and of the Holy Spirit." There is one name. God's name is "Father, Son, and Holy Spirit".

Why when speaking of the three persons in the Godhead, do we always name the Father first, the Son second, and the Holy Spirit third?

The Bible consistently speaks of the Father sending and operating through the Son and the Holy Spirit; also the Bible speaks of the Son as sending and working through the Holy Spirit.

We pray to God

What is prayer?

WSC 98. What is prayer?

Prayer is offering our desires to God in the name of Christ for things that agree with his will, confessing our sins, and thankfully recognizing his mercies.

What is a very simple definition of prayer?

Talking to God

What did Jesus give us to help us learn how to pray?

The Lord's Prayer

What are the five parts of the Lord's Prayer?

- Worship and Adoration
  "Hallowed be thy name"

- Prayer for God's rule
  "Thy kingdom come, thy will be done"

- Prayer for our needs
  "Give us this day our daily bread"

- Prayer for sins to be forgiven
  "Forgive us our debts as we forgive our debtors"

- Prayer for protection and guidance
  "Lead us not into temptation, but deliver us from evil"

Review

Lesson 4 – God is one God who exists in three persons. Although truly one unity, there are tri (three persons) who are equally God in every respect of their being, wisdom, power, holiness, justice, goodness, and truth. Each person of the Trinity (tri-unity): Father, Son, and Holy Spirit are equally infinite, eternal, and unchangeable. Yet there is one God.

Prayer

- Father God – we are very thankful for the privilege of prayer
  - We bring our desires to you in the name of our savior, Jesus who is God
  - We are thankful that God the Holy Spirit encourages and helps us to pray
- Father – we pray as you have taught us to pray:

  Our Father in heaven,

  hallowed be your name.

  your kingdom come,

  your will be done,

  on earth as it is in heaven.

  Give us this day our daily bread.

  And forgive us our debts,

  as we also have forgiven our debtors

  And lead us not into temptation,

  but deliver us from the evil one.

  For yours is the kingdom,

  and the power,

  and the glory forever.

  Amen.

Lesson 5

God's Decrees

How God is Completely in Control of All That Happens

Introduction

We have learned that the one infinite, eternal, and unchangeable God is in three persons. Persons have purposes and make plans. So does God. God is omni-present and omni-powerful and has purposes for every part of his creation. But does God achieve all his purposes?

What is the difference between our plans and what really happens?

A plan is something we intend to happen. Sometimes the results follow our plans, but often they do not.

Why can our plans fail to come about?

- We fail to anticipate and make the wrong plan, which must be abandoned.

- We lack knowledge of how to accomplish the plan.

- We lack power to overcome resistance to our plan.

- We are limited to being in one place at one time and must choose between plans.

- We lack the resolve to complete our plan.

- We change our mind.

We have learned that God is infinitely powerful. What do you think happens when God wants something to happen?

> *It comes to pass. If God's intentions did not come to pass then his desire would be thwarted and thus prove that he is not all-powerful.*

What would it mean if God made a plan and it didn't come about?

> *That failure would indicate that God is somehow limited in knowledge, power, or character.*

From our lesson – what is a decree?

> *A decree is a plan of God that will certainly happen. It is an order that has both authority and force behind it.*

WSC 7. What are the decrees of God"?

The decrees of God are his eternal plan based on the purpose of his will, by which, for his own glory, he has foreordained everything that happens.

How do we as people make plans? What do we base our plans upon?

- We decide what we want based upon what we know.
- We may ask other people what they think.
- We decide what is possible to do.
- We consider the things we will need; we might ask other people to help.
- We select a time when the circumstances would allow us to do it.

Do we ever have to change our plans?

> *Yes. Our plans change and fail all the time.*

How does God make plans? What does he base his plans upon?

He bases his plans on "the purpose of his will." Purposes that are for his pleasure – "I will do all that I please".

We read of God's decrees in Isaiah:

> **Isaiah 46:8-10**
>
> Remember this, fix it in mind, take it to heart, you rebels. 9 Remember the former things, those of long ago; I am God, and there is no other; I am God, and there is none like me. 10 I make known the end from the beginning, from ancient times, what is still to come. I say: My purpose will stand, and I will do all that I please.

According to Isaiah, what do God's plans include?

God's plans include everything, including the future.

Does God ever need to change his plans?

No. His purposes (plans) are unchanging.

Scriptures about God's Decrees	Summary
Psalm 115:33 Our God is in heaven; he does whatever pleases him.	God is sovereign and acts according to his please.
Psalm 135:6 The LORD does whatever pleases him, in the heavens and on the earth, in the seas and all their depths.	God's decrees are fulfilled everywhere.
Revelation 4:11 "You are worthy, our Lord and God, to receive glory and honor and power, for you created all things, and by your will they were created and have their being."	All things exist by God's will.

Ephesians 1:11	Salvation is by
In him we were also chosen, having been predestined according to the plan of him who works out everything in conformity with the purpose of his will.	God's decree.

God's Secret Decrees

Do we know all the plans (decrees) of God?

No. Many of God's plans are not revealed to us. We can only know those secret plans after they come to pass.

Scriptures about God's Secret Decrees	Summary
Deuteronomy 29:29 The secret things belong to the LORD our God, but the things revealed belong to us and to our children forever, that we may follow all the words of this law.	God's secret plans are known to him alone. His moral law is revealed to us.

Decrees and the choices of People

Do God's decrees also include the choices of people?

Yes.

So God's plans include even our sinful choices?

Yes

How does that work?

People are agents. They make choices. They choose according to their nature and desires. However, their choices do not defeat or frustrate God's decrees. Even the evil choices and actions of mankind are within God's total sovereignty. How God is in control of the evil that he hates is part of his secret degrees, and not revealed to us.

God worked out his purposes in the life of Joseph, through the wicked act of his brothers, who sold him into slavery. In fact, this resulted in their good as well as Joseph's.

> **Genesis 50:18-21**
>
> His brothers then came and threw themselves down before him. "We are your slaves," they said. But Joseph said to them, "Don't be afraid. Am I in the place of God? 20 You intended to harm me, but God intended it for good to accomplish what is now being done, the saving of many lives. 21 So then, don't be afraid. I will provide for you and your children." And he reassured them and spoke kindly to them.

God also worked out his plan of redemption through the most heinous act– the crucifixion of Jesus.

> **Acts 2:22-23**
>
> Men of Israel, listen to this: Jesus of Nazareth was a man accredited by God to you by miracles, wonders and signs, which God did among you through him, as you yourselves know. 23 This man was handed over to you by God's set purpose and foreknowledge; and you, with the help of wicked men, put him to death by nailing him to the cross.

Was it in God's plan that Jesus be crucified?

Yes. By God's set purpose and foreknowledge (v 23).

Who put him on the cross?

Wicked men crucified Christ.

Why did they do this?

They sinfully desired it.

Did God make them sin?

No.

Was their sin part of God's plan and decrees?

Yes. But all things are not decreed in the same sense. Sinful acts of men are not decreed in the same sense as righteous acts. God is the cause of all that is good, while evil is rebellion against God. He sovereignly permits for his glory; God decrees the sinful acts of men as part of his sovereign plan. But men in sinning are giving expression to their own inherent depravity.

God and Evil

God is completely righteous and yet rules over evil.

Isn't this a contradiction?

No.

Some people mistakenly believe that it is impossible and illogical that a God who is completely good and powerful would allow evil to exist. Accordingly, they use the existence of evil to deny God's existence.

Indeed, if there were no possible good reason for God to allow evil, we would then have a contradiction. In that case the resolution to the contradiction would be one or more of the following: God does not exist; evil does not exist; or God is limited in power or goodness.

However, Scripture does assert that God has good reasons for decreeing the evil that he hates. God overturns the fall and destroys evil and in so doing demonstrates his goodness and justice. Indeed, evil and suffering are terrible, and God's ways are mysterious to us. We rightly desire and pray for the end of evil. But the existence of evil does not deny God's existence or goodness.

God's Decrees and our Lives

Is becoming a Christian part of God's sovereign plan?

> *Yes. God has decreed our salvation.*

Ephesians 1:4-6

For he chose us in him before the creation of the world to be holy and blameless in his sight. In love 5 he predestined us to be adopted as his sons through Jesus Christ, in accordance with his pleasure and will- 6 to the praise of his glorious grace, which he has freely given us in the One he loves.

How do we know if God has decreed that we be saved?

> *By obeying the command to repent and believe in Christ. Then we can know with confidence that he chose us before the world began.*

As a Christian how does it make you feel to know that God has a plan that will be carried out?

> *It makes us feel secure and confident. Even if we face terrible things, we know that all will work out for our good and God's glory.*

Romans 8:28-30

And we know that in all things God works for the good of those who love him, who have been called according to his purpose. 29 For those God foreknew he also predestined to be conformed to the likeness of his Son, that he might be the firstborn among many brothers. 30 And those he predestined, he also called; those he called, he also justified; those he justified, he also glorified.

Has God decreed where you will be living and what you will be doing in the future?

> *Yes.*

Can you know this decree beforehand?

No. It is not revealed to you.

What does the Bible tell us?

The Bible tells us what we are to believe about God and what he expects of us. What he expects of us is given to us in the commandments of scripture.

Deuteronomy 29:29

The <u>secret things</u> belong to the LORD our God, but the things revealed belong to us and to our children forever, <u>that we may follow all the words of this law</u>.

So how do you make decisions about what to do in life?

- Seek God's glory above all things.

- Follow God's commands in scripture. Marriage is an example. You are commanded to only marry a Christian and a person of the opposite sex.

- Where there is no command – seek wisdom. Use the resources God has provided you – information and good counsel.

- Make a decision and trust God.

- Don't bother trying to guess God's secret will, no one knows that but God – it is his business, not yours.

WSC 8. How does God carry out his decrees?

God carries out his decrees in creation and providence.

WSC 9. With what did God make everything?

The work of creation is the making by God of all things from nothing, by his powerful word, in the space of six days, and all very good.

WSC 10. How did God create man?

God created man, male and female, in his own image and in knowledge, righteousness, and holiness, to rule over the other creatures.

Did man stay this way?

No. By his choice he fell and became sinful. We will study this in the next lesson.

Knowing that God's plans are certain is very practical:

- It magnifies God's wisdom, power, and sovereignty. It puts God on the throne where He should be and is ever and always.

- The believer is humbled at the sight of such a great God, and his soul is bowed in adoring wonder and worship.

- It brings us comfort and security.

- It brings peace in making our decisions according to what God has provided and made known (his moral will) and delivers us from worrying about knowing the future.

Review

Lesson 5 – God is infinite in his knowledge, wisdom, and power. He is also unchangeable and eternal. Accordingly every intention and plan of God is final, eternal, and is realized perfectly. We call his plans decrees. God need not seek advice or counsel to form his decrees, as they are based upon his own good pleasure and are for his own glory. His decrees (plans) include every aspect of his creation and are worked out through his creation and providential care. Even the decisions and actions of men, freely chosen, are mysteriously but absolutely part of God's decrees. God's sovereign secret decrees are not revealed to men through revelation. We are to live our lives by obeying his revealed will, seeking God's glory, pursuing wisdom, and freely choosing our path as we glorify and enjoy God.

<u>Prayer</u>

- Father – we thank you that you are infinite and good in all that you are
    - You are perfect in your being, wisdom, power, holiness, justice, goodness, and truth
    - All of your plans come to pass certainly
    - You are sovereign over everything, even fallen creation and evil deeds
    - You will use all things for your glory and purposes
- Father – Guide us our Lord
    - To obey your commands
    - To trust you in every part of our lives
    - To live out our purpose to glorify you and enjoy you

Lesson 6

Sin

The Fall and Its Consequences

Introduction

Everything we have learned about God creates awe and wonder in us. God is perfection without end or change. But – we look at the world and see a very different picture indeed; it is a picture of brokenness, death, heartache, and frustration. How did this come about and why did God not prevent it? This brings us to the topic of sin and the fall of creation.

God's Creation of Man

> **WSC 10. How did God create man?**
>
> *God created man, male and female, in his own image and knowledge, righteousness, and holiness, to rule over the creatures.*

How are we created in God's image?

> *We have personality, will, reason, and knowledge as God does.*

What is free will?

> *First we must define what the will of a person is. The will of a person is the mind of the person making a choice. More succinctly: the will is the mind choosing.*
>
> *Having a free will is to be free to choose according to who we are, without being forced from the outside. We are free*

to choose according to our nature and the desires that come from that nature.

Does God have free will? Can God make any choice?

Yes. God has free will. As we do, he chooses according to his nature. God chooses according to his holy and perfect nature. God is not free to choose in error or to make an evil choice.

Adam and Eve were part of God's good creation. Why did God give Adam and Eve the ability to disobey and thereby choose evil?

This is not explained in Scripture. We can at most speculate why God made Adam capable of sinning. Many think that for God to create people incapable of sinning would be to create more of a robot than a human person in the image of God. A serious objection to that argument is that Christians in heaven will be image bearers who are incapable of sinning. They will not be robots. So, Adam and Eve's initial sin remains a great mystery. It is part of God's secret decrees.

God's Providence

We learned in the last lesson that one of the ways that God carries out his decrees (plans) is through his Providence.

WSC 11. What are God's works of Providence?

God's providence is his completely holy, wise, and powerful preserving and governing every creature and every action.

How did God provide for Adam and Eve?

- He provided them a wonderful garden to live in.
- He provided them one another – companionship.
- He gave them the garden and the animals to govern.
- He commanded that they multiply and subdue (rule over) the entire earth.

- God made a covenant with man to give him *eternal* life, if he perfectly obeyed. He also told Adam not to eat from the tree of knowledge of good and evil or he would die.

Genesis 1:28

God blessed them and said to them, "Be fruitful and increase in number; fill the earth and subdue it. Rule over the fish of the sea and the birds of the air and over every living creature that moves on the ground."

WSC 12. What special act of providence did God exercise toward man in the state in which he was created?

When God had created man, he entered into a covenant of life with him, on condition of perfect obedience, forbidding him to eat of the tree of the knowledge of good and evil on penalty of death.

Genesis 2:15-17

The LORD God took the man and put him in the Garden of Eden to work it and take care of it. 16 And the LORD God commanded the man, "You are free to eat from any tree in the garden; 17 but you must not eat from the tree of the knowledge of good and evil, for when you eat of it you will surely die."

What was offered Adam and Eve if they obeyed?

Adam was created to experience perfect harmony with God for eternity. God made a covenant with man to give him eternal life, if he perfectly obeyed.

The Fall

The fall of man occurs shortly after the creation of man.

Genesis 3:1-13

Now the serpent was more crafty than any of the wild animals the LORD God had made. He said to the woman, "Did God really say, 'You must not eat from any tree in the garden'?"

2 The woman said to the serpent, "We may eat fruit from the trees in the garden, 3 but God did say, 'You must not eat fruit from the tree that is in the middle of the garden, and you must not touch it, or you will die.'"

4 "You will not surely die," the serpent said to the woman. 5 "For God knows that when you eat of it your eyes will be opened, and you will be like God, knowing good and evil."

6 When the woman saw that the fruit of the tree was good for food and pleasing to the eye, and also desirable for gaining wisdom, she took some and ate it. She also gave some to her husband, who was with her, and he ate it. 7 Then the eyes of both of them were opened, and they realized they were naked; so they sewed fig leaves together and made coverings for themselves.

8 Then the man and his wife heard the sound of the LORD God as he was walking in the garden in the cool of the day, and they hid from the LORD God among the trees of the garden. 9 But the LORD God called to the man, "Where are you?" 10 He answered, "I heard you in the garden, and I was afraid because I was naked; so I hid."

11 And he said, "Who told you that you were naked? Have you eaten from the tree that I commanded you not to eat from?"

12 The man said, "The woman you put here with me – she gave me some fruit from the tree, and I ate it."

> 13 Then the LORD God said to the woman, "What is this you have done?"
>
> The woman said, "The serpent deceived me, and I ate."

What were Adam and Eve's sin and what led to it?

The sin was eating the forbidden fruit. God was very clear that it should not be eaten.

Notice – there are two parts to our sinning:

> *(1) We first question, disregard, or modify God's clear command. In this case Satan caused Eve to question God's command – that the result of eating would not be death but to be like God.*

> *(2) We then lie to ourselves about the sin itself. In this passage Eve embraces the lie that the fruit is pleasing and attractive – rather than off limits.*

WSC 14. What is Sin?

Sin is disobeying God or not conforming to God's law in any way.

How does the sin of Adam and Eve fit this definition?

They disobeyed God's direct command.

What are some examples of disobeying God's law?

Stealing, lying, taking God's name in vain, murdering...

What are some examples of not conforming to God's law?

Not loving God or our neighbor fully. God's law is much more than restrictions. It is a portrait of someone who loves God and others well.

What should we do to combat the temptation to sin?

1. Rehearse

Rehearse in your mind the truth about God. Meditate on God's goodness and commands. Delight in them.

Psalm 119:11

Thy word have I hid in mine heart, that I might not sin against thee.

Psalm 19:7-11 7

The law of the LORD is perfect, reviving the soul.

The statutes of the LORD are trustworthy, making wise the simple. 8 The precepts of the LORD are right, giving joy to the heart.The commands of the LORD are radiant, giving light to the eyes. 9 The fear of the LORD is pure, enduring forever.

The ordinances of the LORD are sure and altogether righteous. 10 They are more precious than gold, than much pure gold; they are sweeter than honey,than honey from the comb. 11 By them is your servant warned; in keeping them there is great reward.

---

2. Request

Be quick to pray to God and bring him praise and requests. As the apostle Paul instructs: pray without ceasing.

Matthew 6:13

And lead us not into temptation, but deliver us from evil:

Mark 14:38

Watch and pray so that you will not fall into temptation. The spirit is willing, but the flesh is weak.

---

3. Repent

Be quick to repent. Do this immediately in prayer and if you can - make your repentance known to other Christians.

> **1 John 1:8-10**
> If we claim to be without sin, we deceive ourselves and the truth is not in us. 9 If we confess our sins, he is faithful and just and will forgive us our sins and purify us from all unrighteousness. 10 If we claim we have not sinned, we make him out to be a liar and his word has no place in our lives.

4. Resist

Temptations to sin and to delay repentance are the devil's work. In the moment of temptation, submit yourself to your loving Heavenly Father, ask for strength, and resist sin.

> **James 4:7**
> Submit yourselves therefore to God. Resist the devil, and he will flee from you.

5. Run

Do not stay in the place of temptation. Do not rely on your own strength to resist when the wise thing to do is to get away.

> **1 Corinthians 10:14**
> Wherefore, my dearly beloved, flee from idolatry.

6. Rejoice

Rejoice in trial. Confess the gospel as true, your Father in heaven as loving and powerful, and your destiny as glorious.

> **Luke 6:23**
> Rejoice in that day and leap for joy, because great is your reward in heaven.

Original Sin

Did the fall of Adam only affect Adam?

WSC 16. Did all mankind fall in Adam's first disobedience?

Since the covenant was made not only for Adam but also for his natural descendants, all mankind sinned in him and fell with him in his first disobedience.

The Bible teaches that Adam represented us all and that his sin affected all of humanity. Just as the President of a country represents the people and his choices affect his people, God appointed that Adam would represent all of mankind. Just as he promised Adam eternal life if he perfectly obeyed, God would also give his descendants eternal life as well. Conversely, when Adam sinned and fell into a condition of sin and misery, so did all of mankind through that single sin of Adam.

Romans 5:12-17

Therefore, just as sin entered the world through one man, and death through sin, and in this way death came to all men, because all sinned- 13 for before the law was given, sin was in the world. But sin is not taken into account when there is no law. 14 Nevertheless, death reigned from the time of Adam to the time of Moses, even over those who did not sin by breaking a command, as did Adam, who was a pattern of the one to come. 15 But the gift is not like the trespass. For if the many died by the trespass of the one man, how much more did God's grace and the gift that came by the grace of the one man, Jesus Christ, overflow to the many! 16 Again, the gift of God is not like the result of the one man's sin: The judgment followed one sin and brought condemnation, but the gift followed many trespasses and brought justification. 17 For if, by the trespass of the one man, death reigned through that one man, how much more will those who receive God's abundant provision of grace and of the gift of righteousness reign in life through the one man, Jesus Christ.

WSC 17. What has happened to man in the fall?

Man fell into a condition of sin and misery.

WSC 18. What is sinful about man's fallen condition)?

The sinfulness of the fallen condition is twofold:

First, in what is commonly called original sin, there is the guilt of Adam's first sin with its lack of original righteousness and the corruption of his whole nature.

Second are all the specific acts of disobedience that come from original sin.

Guilt – We are all guilty from birth because of Adam's sin.

1 Corinthians 15:22
For as in Adam all die, so in Chri*st all will be made alive.*

Lack – We are not born righteous or innocent – we grow up choosing to sin.

Ephesians 2:3
All of us also lived among them at one time, gratifying the cravings of our sinful nature and following its desires and thoughts. Like the rest, we were by nature objects of wrath.

Corruption – Every part of us is corrupted, and everything we do is guided by our sinful nature. We sin because we are sinners.

Romans 3:10-11
There is no one righteous, not even one;   11 there is no one who understands, no one who seeks God.

The Misery of Fallenness

> **WSC 19. What is the misery of Man's fallen condition?**
>
> *By their fall all mankind lost fellowship with God and brought his anger and curse on themselves. They are therefore subject to all the miseries of this life, to death itself, and to the pains of hell forever.*

Result of the Fall	Our Condition
Physical Death	Our bodies stop working and we eventually and certainly die.
Physical Misery	Suffering, sickness, declining strength and vitality, death.
Spiritual Death	Life without God.
Loss of Fellowship with God	Alienation from God and even suppress his truth (Roman 1).
We are objects of God's wrath and punishment	Enemies of God.
Misery and dissatisfaction	Heartache, grieving, loss of purpose, loss of fulfillment.
Eternal Separation	Life eternally apart from God.

Note that there are two types of death that inflict fallen
humanity: physical (our bodies) and spiritual (our relationship
to God).

Fallenness	Type of Death
Ecclesiastes 3:20 All go to the same place; all come from dust, and to dust all return. 21 Who knows if the human spirit rises upward and if the spirit of the animal goes down into the earth?"	Physical and Spiritual
John 11:14 So then he told them plainly, "Lazarus is dead".	Physical
Romans 5:12 Therefore, just as sin entered the world through one man, and death through sin, and in this way death came to all people, because all sinned.	Physical and Spiritual
Romans 6:23 For the wages of sin is death, but the gift of God is eternal life in Christ Jesus our Lord.	Physical
1 Corinthians 15:22 For as in Adam all die, so in Christ all will be made alive. 23 But each in turn: Christ, the first fruits; then, when he comes, those who belong to him.	Physical

Revelation 21:8	Physical and Spiritual
But the cowardly, the unbelieving, the vile, the murderers, the sexually immoral, those who practice magic arts, the idolaters and all liars—they will be consigned to the fiery lake of burning sulfur. This is the second death	

Review of this lesson

Lesson 6 – God created Adam in his own image and in a state of total righteousness. Adam was given a will (the ability to make choices). God was clear in his instruction about the consequences of obedience (Eternal life) and disobedience (death). Adam fell because he did not glorify God through obedience. The results were guilt, lack, corruption, and death for Adam and all mankind. Because of Adam's fall, all mankind fell. This is called original sin.

Prayer

- Father – these are sad and terrible truths that we have studied.
    - Adam, the representative of mankind, sinned and brought death and corruption to all
    - Sin is real and devastating – we see its affects in ourselves and in the entire world.
    - Sin results in physical, mental, and spiritual death and misery
    - We are sinful and deserving of your judgment
- Father – our earnest prayer is that you would deliver us from evil
    - That we would honor and glorify and enjoy you
    - That we would be forgiven because of Christ
    - That you would cleanse us from our unrighteousness
    - That our fellowship with you would be strong
    - That we would quick to grieve over sin and to repent of it.

Lesson 7
The Law of God
God Reveals his Moral Standard

Introduction

Sin is disobeying God in any way. We have learned how Adam's disobedience (the fall) resulted in guilt and corruption and death for all of mankind. Therefore, all of mankind became morally corrupt after the fall. We lost our true purpose, which is to love and glorify God (lesson 1). In revealing his moral standards to us through his moral law, God informs us of our fallen condition, teaches us more of what it means to love him, restrains evil, and prepares us for the way of salvation.

What is the second thing that the Bible teaches (WSC 3)?

What God requires of man

Why do we owe obedience to God?

Because God is our creator and we are his creatures. We are under a moral obligation to love and serve him.

WSC 39. What does God require of man?

God requires man to obey his revealed will.

WSC 40. What were the rules, which God first revealed for man to obey?

The rules he first revealed were the moral law.

How was the moral law given to mankind in the state of innocence (Adam and Eve before the fall)?

Mankind was created with the moral law of God written upon their hearts and minds. It was not necessary for God to address Adam and Eve with a special revelation of the moral law for God already wrote it in their nature. This changed when the fall occurred and the human conscience was darkened.

Who must obey God's moral law?

Every human being that has ever lived.

Does the person who knows nothing of the Bible need to obey the moral law of God? How?

Yes. They must obey the moral law written upon their consciences and as received in God's natural revelation. See Romans 1 and Romans 2:14-16.

Does the moral law require us to be good?

Yes. But we are not only required to be good, but morally perfect. That is, we must love God completely with all of our being and completely live to glorify and enjoy him in every aspect of our lives.

WSC 41. Where is the moral law set out briefly?

The moral law is set out briefly in the Ten Commandments.

WSC 42. What is the essence of the Ten Commandments?

Love. The essence of the Ten Commandments is to love the Lord our God with all our heart, with all our soul, with all our strength and with our entire mind. And to love everyone else as we love ourselves.

Can eternal life be obtained in any other way than by the fulfilling of God's moral law?

No. The moral law will never pass away.

What about the gospel, is that not another way to eternal life?

Christ, the second Adam, perfectly fulfilled the moral law on our behalf through a perfect life and by bearing the penalty of our not obeying God's moral law. Hence the gospel does not lower the standard of obedience. Rather than the law being removed for us, it is fulfilled for us.

If the moral law cannot save us, of what use it is to all mankind?

a) It reveals the truth about God.

b) It reveals the truth of our obligation to God.

c) It convinces us of our utterly sinful condition.

d) It helps us understand the matchless character of Christ.

How does the moral law serve to awaken the conscience of the non-Christian?

By declaring the wrath of God that is against all unrighteousness. This stirs up the conscience to be afraid of the judgment of God that is coming upon them.

Romans 1:18

The wrath of God is being revealed from heaven against all the godlessness and wickedness of people, who suppress the truth by their wickedness.

Does *the moral law provide a way of escape from the wrath of God?*

No. God's standard is perfection and no amount of striving to obey it will result in the removal of God's wrath.

Does the moral law awaken the conscience of all sinners and lead them to Christ for forgiveness?

No. The knowledge of the moral law must be accompanied by the proclamation of the Gospel of Christ and the work of the Holy Spirit.

Acts 16:14

One of those listening was a woman from the city of Thyatira named Lydia, a dealer in purple cloth. She was a worshiper of God. The Lord opened her heart to respond to Paul's message.

Should a Christian be afraid to commit a sin?

Yes.

Should a Christian be afraid to commit a sin because of the danger of eternal condemnation?

No. The fear of the Christian to sin is the fear of a child who does not want to disobey and dishonor their loving father. It is not a fear based upon the possibility of rejection or hostility.

---
1 John 4:18

There is no fear in love. But perfect love drives out fear, because fear has to do with punishment. The one who fears is not made perfect in love.

Why should a Christian take great care to obey the moral law of God?

Because the law of God summarizes what it means to honor God and to love him. It is the way to live out our God given purpose of glorifying and enjoying God.

For how long will the Christian need to obey the moral law of God?

For all eternity – obeying the moral law of God will never pass away. It will always be a glorious blessing to worship God through obedience to his revealed will. Certain specific commands apply to our life on earth (obeying earthly authorities for example, or faithfulness in marriage) and these will not be relevant in heaven. But many aspects of God's law will continue for all eternity (worshipping the one true God, loving him with all that we are, not taking his name in vain, etc.)

The Ten Commandments

Again, the Ten Commandments summarize the moral law of God.

What were the circumstances of God giving the Ten Commandments?

The nation of Israel was travelling through the desert from Egypt towards the Promised Land. The 10 Commandments were given at the mountain of Sinai and were accompanied by great and fearful signs of God's glory (smoke, blaring trumpets, etc..). The people were made afraid so that they would fear and obey God.

How did God introduce the Ten Commandments? What is this called?

> **Exodus 20:1-2**
>
> And God spoke all these words: 2 "I am the Lord your God, who brought you out of Egypt, out of the land of slavery.

This is called "The Preface"

What is the "first table" of the Law?

The first table of the law contains the commandments about our relationship and duties to God, and how to love him.

What is the "second table" of the Law?

The second table of the law contains the commandments about our relationship to other people, and our duty to love them as our neighbor.

Are the Ten Commandments a complete statement of the moral law?

Not every command of God is specifically listed within the Ten Commandments. But, they are a complete summary of the moral law of God.

Are the two tables of the moral law equally important?

Yes – every command must be obeyed and to transgress any one is to transgress the whole. But, the basis of the second table is the first table. In other words, our moral responsibility to God is the basis of our duties to our fellow men. The first and greatest commandment is to love God, and our duty to love our neighbor emerges naturally and appropriately from our duty to love God.

What two things does each commandment teach?

What is required.

What is forbidden.

Where can we find a summary of what is required and forbidden for each commandment?

In the Shorter Catechism questions 45-81.

The questions of the Shorter Catechism are very helpful in understanding each commandment. The Larger Catechism provides a more expanded explanation.

A Review of the Ten Commandments

	Topic	Command	Required	Forbidden
First Table - How to Love God				
1	**Religion**	You shall have no other gods before me (before my face).	To know, recognize, worship, and glorify only the LORD God.	Not worshipping God or to give worship or glory to any thing.
2	**Worship**	You shall not make for yourselves any graven images.	To keep perfectly all regulations for worship that are in God's word.	Worshipping God with images or any other way that he has not established.

3	**Reverence**	You shall not take the name of the LORD your God in vain.	The holy and reverent use of God's name, title, qualities, regulations, word, and works.	Treating as unholy anything God uses to make himself known.
4	**Rest**	Remember the Sabbath Day to keep it holy.	To set apart to God the times God has set apart in his word – specifically the Sabbath day.	Treating the Sabbath as unholy by neglect or by unnecessary attention to worldly affairs.
Second Table – How to Love your Neighbor				
5	**Authority**	Honor your father and your mother.	To respect and honor people who are in proper authority over us.	To disrespect those in proper authority.
6	**Life**	You shall not murder.	To make every lawful effort to preserve our own life and the lives of others.	Taking one's own life or the lives of others unjustly or doing anything that leads to suicide or murder.
7	**Marriage**	You shall not commit adultery.	Requires everyone to keep sexually pure in heart,	Thinking, saying, or doing anything

			speech, and action.	sexually impure.
8	**Property**	You shall not steal.	That we *lawfully* acquire and increase our money and possessions.	Anything that unjustly takes away money or possessions from another.
9	**Truth**	You shall not bear false witness.	To tell the truth. To maintain and promote truth. To be true in our words and safeguard our reputation.	Anything that gets in the way of truth or injures another's reputation.
10	**Heart**	You shall not covet.	To be completely satisfied with our own status in life and to have a proper loving attitude toward others and their possessions.	Any dissatisfaction with what belongs to us, such as envy or grief at the success of others. Any improper desire for anything that belongs to someone else.

Do you see that the Ten Commandments summarize the moral law of God? Can you think of a sin that does not come under one of these commands?

Every sin seems to fit within the principles of God's moral law as summarized in the Ten Commandments.

Example sins and their basis in the Ten Commandments

Sin	Essence of the Sin	Commandment(s)
Atheism	Lack of Worship, Idolatry	1,2
Self Absorption	Worship of Self	1
Despair	Total mistrust in God	1
Preaching our own thoughts	Worship not commanded by God	2
Worshipping man made images of God	Improper representations of God	2
Swearing	Lack of reverence	3
Misusing Scripture	Lack of reverence	3
Praying to saints	Improper worship, reverence	1,2,3
Absorption with end times	Improper reverence	3
Sunday as regular work day	Not keeping the Sabbath	4
Speeding on the freeway	Not observing proper authority	5
Abortion	Not preserving life	6

Sexually explicit music videos	Sexual Impurity	7
Shady advertising	Unlawful gain	8
Gossip	Damaging another's reputation	9
Undue focus on wealth	Dissatisfaction with our life	10

Review

Lesson 7 – The Bible teaches what God requires of man. Every person must obey God's revealed will to attain eternal life. God reveals his nature and will in his natural creation and in his revelation to us through scripture. The moral law of God is summarized in the Ten Commandments. The Ten Commandments comprehensively summarize our duty to love God totally and our neighbor as we do ourselves.

Prayer

- Father – you have told us how we should live
  - o You have given us your moral law as summarized in the 10 Commandments
  - o Your law tells us how we are to love and honor God and how we are to love other people
  - o Your law tells us what is required and what is forbidden
  - o Every command you give deserves our full obedience
  - o Every sin we can commit, of both omission and commission, can be found within the summary that is the 10 Commandments
  - o You rightly condemn any transgression of your moral law
- Father – thank you that you have provided Jesus as our Savior – who has perfectly kept the law for us and paid the penalty for our disobedience
- Father – help us to live out your law of love with all that we are, loving and honoring both god and neighbor

Lesson 8

Jesus and the Covenant of Grace

God's Solution to Man's Huge Problem

Introduction

In the last lesson we discussed God's moral law. God's first declaration of his moral law was to Adam when he commanded him not to eat of the tree of the knowledge of good and evil. This commandment also constituted a covenant (a sacred agreement) with Adam and all his descendants. Adam sinned and broke this covenant, resulting in the fall and misery of mankind. A new covenant is God's gracious response to the fall of mankind.

Why is the covenant with Adam (and all mankind through Adam) called the Covenant of Works?

Because it was an arrangement made by God, which formed the basis of how mankind could gain eternal life; that is, by works of obedience to God.

There is another name that is given to the Covenant of Works. Can you guess what that is?

*The means of fulfilling the covenant was Adam's righteousness. The result of fulfilling the covenant was eternal life for Adam and all of mankind. Hence, the covenant is also called: the **Covenant of Life**.*

What was the result of Adam's failure to keep the Covenant of Works (Life)?

Death - for Adam and all mankind.

WSC 17. What has happened to man in the fall?

Man fell into a condition of sin and misery.

WSC 18. What is sinful about man's fallen condition?

The sinfulness of the fallen condition is twofold:

First, in what is commonly called original sin, there is the guilt of Adam's first sin with its lack of original righteousness and the corruption of his whole nature.

Second are all the specific acts of disobedience that come from original sin.

WSC 19. What is the misery of man's fallen condition?

By their fall all mankind lost fellowship with God and brought his anger and curse on themselves. They are therefore subject to all the miseries of this life, to death itself, and to the pains of hell forever.

Does it seem fair to you that Adam represented you and that by his fall you are fallen too?

We are represented in life in many ways. Those in authority represent us and make decisions for which we bear the consequences. Examples include parents, government officials, doctors, etc.. It is true that we often resent our representatives, especially when we question their skill or character.

In Adam's case he was created righteous and worthy to representing mankind. We can be confident that God was all wise and knowing in appointing Adam.

The Covenant of Grace

WSC 20. Did God leave all mankind to perish in the state of sin and misery?

God, solely out of his love and mercy, from all eternity elected some to everlasting life, and entered into a covenant of grace to deliver them out of the state of sin and misery, and to bring them into a state of salvation by a Redeemer.

After the fall, was the covenant of works still in place? Why?

>   *No. Adam's sin resulted in the fall of the whole human race
>   and God's requirement of obedience was broken for all
>   mankind.*

Can anyone after Adam attain eternal life by holy living?

>   *No. We are guilty in Adam (Original Sin) even if we were
>   never to commit a sin of our own. Furthermore, each of us
>   is corrupt in our own nature and we do fail to observe the
>   moral law of God in countless ways. We are sinners.*

**When in the Genesis account do we see God revealing a
second covenant?**

Genesis 3:13-15

Then the LORD God said to the woman, "What is this you
have done?" The woman said, "The serpent deceived me, and I
ate."

14 So the LORD God said to the serpent, "Because you have
done this, "Cursed are you above all the livestock and all the
wild animals! You will crawl on your belly and you will eat
dust all the days of your life. 15 And I will put enmity between
you and the woman, and between your offspring and hers; he
will crush your head, and you will strike his heel."

Immediately after the fall God declares punishment upon Adam,
Eve, and the serpent. The serpent is condemned to be crushed
by the offspring of Eve. In crushing the serpent this offspring of
Eve will be injured by the serpent.

**Of the Bible's 1089 chapters – 1086 (after Genesis chapter
three) are under the over the Covenant of Grace!**

Who is the offspring of Eve?

>   *It is Christ Jesus. Our Savior came to fulfill the covenant of
>   works for his people and to bear the penalty of death on our
>   behalf. We see this in many Scriptures, including these:*

> **Galatians 4:4-6**
> But when the time had fully come, God sent his Son, born of a woman, born under law, 5 to redeem those under law, that we might receive the full rights of sons.
>
> **Romans 16:20**
> The God of peace will soon crush Satan under your feet.
>
> **1 John 3:7-9**
> Dear children, do not let anyone lead you astray. He who does what is right is righteous, just as he is righteous. 8 He who does what is sinful is of the devil, because the devil has been sinning from the beginning. The reason the Son of God appeared was to destroy the devil's work.

What is this second covenant called?

The Covenant of Grace

With whom was the Covenant of Grace made?

God made this covenant with Christ.

Comparison of the Two Covenants:

Aspects	Covenant of Works	Covenant of Grace
Who made the covenant?	God	God the Father
With whom was it made?	Adam	Christ
Who was represented?	All mankind	God's people
What was required?	Adam's Work	Christ's Work
What was promised?	Eternal Life	Eternal Life

What was threatened?	Death	Nothing. God the Father and Son were in covenant

When was the Covenant of Grace made?

The covenant of grace was made before the Covenant of Works – before the creation of the world. This shows us that God foreknew the fall and graciously prepared the way of redemption.

Ephesians 1:3-10

Praise be to the God and Father of our Lord Jesus Christ, who has blessed us in the heavenly realms with every spiritual blessing in Christ. 4 <u>For he chose us in him before the creation of the world to be holy and blameless in his sight</u>. In love 5 he predestined us to be adopted as his sons through Jesus Christ, in accordance with his pleasure and will- 6 to the praise of his glorious grace, which he has freely given us in the One he loves. 7 In him we have redemption through his blood, the forgiveness of sins, in accordance with the riches of God's grace 8 that he lavished on us with all wisdom and understanding. 9 And he made known to us the mystery of his will according to his good pleasure, which he purposed in Christ, 10 to be put into effect when the times will have reached their fulfillment-to bring all things in heaven and on earth together under one head, even Christ.

What is grace?

Grace is favor that is not deserved. God's grace gives love and favor, to those, who because of sin deserve his wrath and curse.

Were the Jews of the Old Testament saved by the Covenant of Works or the Covenant of Grace?

> *Some today say that the Covenant of Works remained in place until Calvary. But, this is incorrect. Immediately after the fall the Covenant of Grace was in effect, and righteousness and salvation are obtained only through the work of the seed of the woman – Christ, the second Adam.*

WLC 34. How was the Covenant of Grace administered under the Old Testament?

By promises, prophecies, sacrifices, circumcision, the Passover, and other types and ordinances, which all fore-signify Christ then to come, and were for that time sufficient to build up the elect in faith in the promised Messiah, by whom they had full remission of sin, and eternal salvation.

Redemption

So how does the Covenant of Grace work? Does God merely choose to forgive?

> *The Covenant of Grace provides salvation to fallen men by satisfying the moral law of God and the penalty of sin for them.*

God's justice must be satisfied as He provides grace and mercy. How is this done?

> *Christ satisfies justice and provides mercy by living the perfect live we should have lived and paying the penalty of death for our sin. This is the Gospel!*

What do these terms mean: Redemption, Redeemer, and Ransom?

> *Throughout the Old Testament the Jews are pointed to place their hope and trust in the coming Messiah Redeemer. The Redeemer would rescue his people by paying the price of their salvation. Hence redemption means to be rescued or delivered through the payment of a price. The price paid is called the ransom. A ransom is a price paid to free someone*

from captivity. The redeemer pays the ransom to the one who holds the person in captivity.

Who is in captivity?

Humanity.

How is humanity held in captivity?

It is a captivity of sin, misery, and death (in all its dimensions: physical, mental, and spiritual).

How did humanity get in this condition?

It was by Adam's failure to fulfill the Covenant of Works – the fall.

What ransom price must be paid to God?

The price is perfect obedience to the moral law as well as payment of the sin debt, which is death.

Could any normal human being pay this ransom?

No. All descendants of Adam are guilty in Adam and also in their own sinful behavior. They are subject to Adam's failure to keep the Covenant of Works on their behalf, and are themselves corrupted and break the Moral Law of God.

Christ pays the ransom. He is the mediator of the Covenant of Grace. He is the redeemer.

Ephesians 2 provides us a wonderful look at redemption:

Ephesians 2:1-10

As for you, you were dead in your transgressions and sins, 2 in which you used to live when you followed the ways of this world and of the ruler of the kingdom of the air, the spirit who is now at work in those who are disobedient. 3 All of us also lived among them at one time, gratifying the cravings of our sinful nature and following its desires and thoughts. Like the rest, we were by nature objects of wrath. 4 But because of his great love for us, God, who is rich in mercy, 5 made us alive with Christ even when we were dead in transgressions-it is by grace you have been saved. 6 And God raised us up with Christ and seated us with him in the heavenly realms in Christ Jesus, 7 in order that in the coming ages he might show the incomparable riches of his grace, expressed in his kindness to us in Christ Jesus. 8 For it is by grace you have been saved, through faith-and this not from yourselves, it is the gift of God-9 not by works, so that no one can boast. 10 For we are God's workmanship, created in Christ Jesus to do good works, which God prepared in advance for us to do.

What were we before our conversion?

Dead in our transgressions and sins.

Who were we following?

The ways of the world and Satan.

What were we doing?

Gratifying the desires of our sinful nature.

What were we to God?

We were by nature (original and practical sin) objects of God's wrath.

What did God to?

God made us alive with Christ.

What does it mean that we were dead in transgressions?

We were dead to God, with no desire to glorify and enjoy him; we were alienated from our God given purpose.

Romans 3:9-18

We have already made the charge that Jews and Gentiles alike are all under sin. 10 As it is written: "There is no one righteous, not even one; 11 there is no one who understands, no one who seeks God. 12 All have turned away, they have together become worthless; there is no one who does good, not even one." 13 "Their throats are open graves; their tongues practice deceit." "The poison of vipers is on their lips." 14 "Their mouths are full of cursing and bitterness." 15 "Their feet are swift to shed blood; 16 ruin and misery mark their ways, 17 and the way of peace they do not know." 18 "There is no fear of God before their eyes."

Did we do anything to deserve being made alive by God?

No. It was by grace. This is an entirely undeserved gift from God.

What did God save us to be and to do?

- *To be seated with him – we were once enemies and orphans, now we are sons and daughters who belong to his royal family.*

- *To glorify God by showing his incomparable grace.*

- *To honor God with good works, which he has prepared for us to do.*

Review

Lesson 8 – The Covenant of Works was an arrangement made by God, which formed the basis of how mankind could gain eternal life by works of obedience to God. The Covenant of Works was the representative of mankind Adam. He was promised eternal life for himself and his descendants if he obeyed and death and alienation if he disobeyed. The Covenant of Works is also called the Covenant of Life.

The Covenant of Grace was made in eternity past between God and his son Jesus. The Covenant of Grace established that righteousness and salvation was only obtained through the work of the seed of the woman – Christ the second Adam. Immediately after the fall it was revealed in that the descendent of Eve would conquer Satan and death and would be wounded in doing so.

Christ our Redeemer purchases his people by paying the purchase price (ransom) of perfect obedience to God's moral law and by baring the penalty of our sin for us, which is death. This is a free gift. We are saved by grace alone by faith alone because of Christ alone.

Prayer

- Father – although we are sinners, deserving of your wrath and condemnation, you have provided a Covenant of Grace with us

    o You have provided a Redeemer – our Lord Christ Jesus

    o Jesus has paid the penalty of death for us and lived the perfect life that we should have lived to honor and glorify you

    o You have delivered us from captivity to sin, misery, and death

    o You have redeemed us and made us alive to God

- Father – we praise you and thank you for providing Jesus for us so that by faith we can know that we are "In Christ" rather than "In Adam" and can live to glorify and enjoy you as our Heavenly Father.

Lesson 9

Jesus – His Person and Work

Salvation is by Christ Alone

Introduction

Jesus fulfills the Covenant of Grace. He is the only one who could be the Redeemer. His unique and powerful work of redemption was intimately tied to his matchless person.

> **WSC 21. Who is the redeemer of God's chosen ones?**
>
> *The only redeemer of God's chosen is the Lord Jesus Christ, the eternal Son of God, Who became man. He was and continues to be God and man in two distinct natures and one person forever.*

This catechism question teaches us:

- There is only one redeemer for mankind- Jesus.

- Those who are redeemed are chosen by God

- God the Son became a man – though he was not always a man.

- Jesus continues to be both a man and God to this day and will remain so forever.

- Jesus has two natures: God and man. Yet he is one person.

The Names of Christ

- He is God: Emmanuel
- He is the Savior: Jesus
- He is the Anointed One: Messiah or Christ

Name	Meaning
Emmanuel	Since Jesus is God (El) the Son. An angel (Matt. 1:23) correctly called him Emmanuel (Hebrew, 'immanu'el), meaning El (god) with us.
	Isaiah 7:14-15 *Therefore the Lord himself will give you a sign: The virgin will be with child and will give birth to a son, and will call him Immanuel.*
Jesus	Jesus or Joshua comes from the Hebrew Yeshua or Yehoshua which means "Jehovah saves."
	Matthew 1:21 *She will give birth to a son, and you are to give him the name Jesus, because he will save his people from their sins.*
Messiah or Christ	Messiah comes from the Hebrew Meshiach, "Anointed One." Greek for Messiah is "Christos" or in English: "Christ". Thus, Jesus Christ joins a name and a title, and means "Jesus the Messiah".
	John 1:41 *The first thing Andrew did was to find his brother Simon and tell him, "We have found the Messiah" (that is, the Christ).*

Names in Scripture, referring to Jesus.

Note how these names reflect Jesus being God, Savior, and Lord.

1. Adam, the Last
   (1 Cor. 15:45)
2. Advocate
   (1 Jn. 2:1)
3. All & in All
   (Col. 3:11)
4. Almighty
   (Rev. 1:8)
5. Altogether Lovely One
   (Song of Sol. 5:16)
6. Amen
   (Rev. 3:14)
7. Anchor
   (Heb. 6:19)
8. Ancient of Days
   (Dan. 7:9-11 with Rev. 1:13-16)
9. Angel [of the Lord]
   (Gen. 16:9-14; Gen. 48:16)
10. Anointed
    (Ps. 2:2).
11. Apostle
    (Heb. 3:1)
12. Arm of the Lord
    (Isa. 53:1)
13. Alpha & Omega
    (Rev. 1:8; 21:6)
14. Author
    (Heb. 12:2)
15. Balm of Gilead
    (Jer. 8:22)
16. Beginning
    (Col. 1:18)
17. Begotten (Only)
    John 3:16)
18. Beloved
    (Eph. 1:6)
19. Bishop of your souls
    (1 Pet. 2:25)
20. Blessed Potentate
    (1 Tim. 6:15)
21. Branch
    (Isa. 11:1; Jer. 23:5; Zech. 3:8; 6:12; Rev. 11:1)
22. Bread
    (John 6:32-33; 6:35)
23. Bridegroom
    (Mt. 9:15; Jn. 3:29; Rev. 21:9)
24. Bright & Morning Star
    (Num. 24:17)
25. Brightness of his (God's) glory
    (Heb. 1:3)

26. Captain of their
    salvation
    (Heb. 2:12; Josh. 5:4)

27. Carpenter ['s son]
    (Mt. 13:55; Mk. 6:3)

28. Chief of 10,000
    Song of Sol. 5:10)

29. Child
    (Isa. 9:6; Mt. 2:8-21)

30. Chosen of God
    (Lk. 23:35)

31. Christ
    (Mt. 1:17; Mk. 8:29;
    Jn. 1:41; Rom. 1:16;
    1 Cor. 1:23)

32. Comforter
    (Isa. 61:2; Jn. 14:16)

33. Commander
    (Isa. 55:4)

34. Consolation of Israel
    (Lk. 2:25)

35. Cornerstone
    (Eph. 2:20; see also
    Isa. 28:16)

36. Counsellor
    (Isa. 9:6; Isa. 40:13)

37. Creator of all things
    (Col. 1:16)

38. Dayspring from on
    high
    (Lk. 1:78)

39. Day Star
    (2 Pet. 1:19)

40. Deliverer
    (Rom. 11:26)

41. Desire of all nations
    (Hag. 2:7)

42. Door
    (Jn. 10:7, 9)

43. Emmanuel
    (Mt. 1:23; see also
    Isa. 7:14; 8:8)

44. End (culmination)
    (Rom 10:4)

45. Express image of his
    (God's) person
    (Heb. 1:3)

46. Faithful Witness
    (Rev. 1:5; 3:14;
    19:11)

47. Faithful & True
    (Rev. 19:11)

48. Father of Eternity
    (Isa. 9:6)

49. Fellow of God (Zech.
    13:7)

50. First & the Last (Rev.
    1:17)

51. First begotten of the
    dead
    (Rev. 1:5)

52. Firstborn (of the
    dead)
    (1 Cor. 15:20, 23)

53. Foundation
    (Isa. 28:16; 1 Cor.
    3:11)

54. Fountain
    (Jer. 2:13; Zech.
    13:1)

55. Forerunner
(Heb. 6:20)

56. Friend of sinners
(Mt. 11:19; Lk. 7:34)

57. Fulness of the
Godhead
(Col. 2:9)

58. Gift of God
(Jn. 4:10; 2 Cor.
9:15)

59. Glory of God
(Isa. 60:1)

60. God
(Jn. 1:1; Mt. 1:23;
Rom. 9:5; 1 Tim.
3:16; Heb. 1:8)

61. Good Master
(Mt. 19:16)

62. Governor
(Mt. 2:6)

63. Great High Priest
(Heb. 4:14)

64. Guide
(Ps. 48:14)

65. Head (of the body)
(Eph. 4:15)

66. Heir of all things
(Heb. 1:2)

67. Helper
(Heb. 13:6)

68. Hiding Place
(Isa. 32:2)

69. High Priest
(Heb. 3:1; 7:1)

70. Holy Child
(Acts 4:30)

71. Holy One (Acts 2:27;
3:14)

72. Hope of Israel
(Jer. 17:3)

73. Horn of salvation
(Ps. 18:2; Lk. 1:69)

74. I AM (Jn. 8:24, 58)

75. Image of God
(2 Cor. 4:4; Col.
1:15)

76. Intercessor
(Heb. 7:25)

77. Jehovah
(Isa. 26:4; 40:3)

78. Jesus
(Mt. 1:21)

79. Judge
(Micah 5:1; Acts
10:42)

80. Just One
(Acts 7:52)

81. Kernal of Wheat (Jn.
12:24)

82. King
(Zech. 14:16)

83. Kinsman
(Ruth 2:14)

84. Lamb of God
(Jn. 1:29, 36; 1 Pet
1:19; Rev. 5:6, 12;
7:17)

85. Last
(Rev. 22:13)

86. Lawgiver
(Isa. 33:22)

87. Life
(1 Jn. 1:2)

88. Light
(Jn. 12:35)

89. Lion of the tribe of
Judah
(Rev. 5:5)

90. Lord & Saviour
(1 Cor. 12:3; 2 Pet.
1:11), see also
Master.

91. Man
(Jn. 19:5; Acts 17:31;
1 Tim. 2:5). See also
Son of Man.

92. Master
(Mt. 8:19)

93. Mediator
(1 Tim. 2:5)

94. Merciful High Priest
(Heb. 2:17)

95. Mercy Seat
(Rom. 3:24-25)

96. Messiah
(Dan. 9:25; Jn. 1:41;
4:25)

97. Mighty God
(Isa. 9:6; 63:1)

98. Minister of the
Sanctuary
(Heb. 8:2)

99. Nazarene
(Mk. 1:24)

100. Nobleman
(Lk. 19:12)

101. Offering
(Eph. 5:2; Heb.
10:10)

102. Offspring of David
(Rev. 22:16)

103. Ointment poured
forth
(Song of Sol. 1:3)

104. Omega
(Rev. 1:8; 21:6)

105. Only Son
(John 3:16)

106. Passover
(1 Cor. 5:7)

107. Peace
(Eph. 2:14)

108. Physician
(Mt. 9:12; Lk. 4:23)

109. Plant of Renown
(Ezek. 34:29)

110. Potentate
(Acts 3:15; 5:31)

111. Prophet
(Acts 3:22-23)

112. Propitiation
(1 Jn. 2:2; 4:10)

113. Power of God
(1 Cor. 1:24)

114. Priest
(Heb. 4:14)

115. Quickening Spirit
(1 Cor. 15:45)

116. Rabbi
(Jn. 3:2; Mt. 26:25;
Jn. 20:16)

117. Ransom
(1 Tim. 2:6)

118. Redeemer,
Redemption
(Isa. 59:20; 60:16; 1
Cor. 1:30)

119. Refuge
(Isa. 25:4)

120. Resurrection & the
Life
(Jn. 11:25)

121. Righteousness
(Jer. 23:6; 33:16; 1
Cor. 1:30)

122. Rock [of offence]
(Deut. 32:15; 1 Cor.
10:4; Rom. 9:33; 1
Pet. 2:8)

123. Rod
(Isa. 11:1)

124. Root
(Rev. 22:16)

125. Rose of Sharon
(Song of Sol. 2:1)

126. Sacrifice
(Eph. 5:2)

127. Sanctification
(1 Cor. 1:30)

128. Savior
(Lk. 1:47; 2:11; 1 Jn.
4:14)

129. Seed of Abraham
(Gal. 3:16, 19)

130. Seed Servant
(Isa. 42:1; 49:5-7;
Mt. 12:18)

131. Shadow of a great
Rock
(Isa. 32:2)

132. Shepherd
(1 Peter 5:4)

133. Shiloh
(Gen. 49:10)

134. Son
(Isa. 9:6; 1 Jn. 4:14)

135. Sower
(Mt. 13:37)

136. Star
(Num. 24:17)

137. Stone
(Psalm 118:22)

138. Sun of
Righteousness
(Mal. 4:2)

139. Surety
(Heb. 7:22)

140. Teacher
(Mt. 26:18; Jn. 3:2;
11:28). See also
Master.

141. Tender Plant
(Isa. 53:2)

142. True Bread
(John 6:32-33; 6:35)

143. Truth
(Jn. 14:6)

144. Vine
    (Jn. 15:1, 5)
145. Way
    (Jn. 14:6)

146. Wisdom [of God]
    (1 Cor. 1:24, 30)
147. Wonderful
    (Isa. 9:6)

How long has Jesus been God?

Jesus has been God the Son from all eternity and will always be the Son of God.

WSC 22. How did Christ, the Son of God, become man?

Christ, the Son of God, became man by assuming a real body and a reasoning soul. He was conceived by the power of the Holy Spirit in the womb of the Virgin Mary, who gave birth to him, yet he was sinless.

Jesus is sent to redeem

Galatians 4:4-7

But when the time had fully come, God sent his Son, born of a woman, born under law, 5 to redeem those under law, that we might receive the full rights of sons. 6 Because you are sons, God sent the Spirit of his Son into our hearts, the Spirit who calls out, "Abba, Father." 7 So you are no longer a slave, but a son; and since you are a son, God has made you also an heir.

What does it mean that Christ assumed a reasoning soul?

Christ took on a human soul with its capacity to think and reason.

What is the difference between the human nature of Jesus and our own?

Our human nature is fallen and sinful. We are born in trespasses and sin, with a sinful heart and a tendency to commit sin. But Jesus was born by the miracle working power of the Holy Spirit with a sinless human nature. He was born without the stain of original sin, and has never committed any transgressions.

> **Luke 1:35 35**
>
> The angel answered, "The Holy Spirit will come upon you, and the power of the Most High will overshadow you. So the holy one to be born will be called the Son of God.

Since Mary, the mother of Jesus, was a sinner like other people, how could Jesus, her son, be born with a sinless human nature?

This was a special miracle, accomplished by the almighty power of God. Only by the supernatural power of God could Mary's child be born with a perfectly sinless heart and nature.

How long will the Son of God continue to be man?

The Son of God has been man since his conception by the Holy Spirit in the womb of Mary, and will continue to be fully God and fully man for all eternity to come.

Why could not an ordinary human being act as the mediator and save humans from sin?

All ordinary human beings are sinners, in need of salvation themselves.

Could God have provided a sinless human being, but not God incarnate?

Even a sinless human being could, at most, have been a substitute for one sinner. Only Christ as God and Man could have the infinite value sufficient to redeem the many.

Why was it necessary that our Savior possess a human nature?

Because to redeem the human race the Redeemer must act as the representative of human beings. Remember that the Covenant of Works was a covenant between God and Adam with the stipulation that if Adam obeyed the moral law he and his descendants would receive eternal life. When Adam disobeyed, he and all humanity fell, and were sentenced to misery and death. Christ is both the descendant of Adam the second Adam who pays our debt of obedience and our penalty of death.

Passages about Christ	Showing his Nature
Matthew 8:24 Without warning, a furious storm came up on the lake, so that the waves swept over the boat. But Jesus was sleeping.	Human
Matthew 8:25-27 The disciples went and woke him, saying, "Lord, save us! We're going to drown!" 26 He replied, "You of little faith, why are you so afraid?" Then he got up and rebuked the winds and the waves, and it was completely calm. 27 The men were amazed and asked, "What kind of man is this? Even the winds and the waves obey him!".	Divine
Matthew 12:46 While Jesus was still talking to the crowd, his mother and brothers stood outside, wanting to speak to him.	Human
Matthew 14:19-21 And he directed the people to sit down on the grass. Taking the five loaves and the two fish and looking up to heaven, he gave thanks and broke the loaves. Then he gave them to the disciples, and the disciples gave them to the people. 20 They all ate and were satisfied, and the disciples picked up twelve basketfuls of broken pieces that were left over. 21 The number of those who ate was about five thousand men, besides women and children.	Divine
Matthew 8:1-4 When he came down from the mountainside, large crowds followed him. 2 A man with leprosy came and knelt before him and said,	Divine

"Lord, if you are willing, you can make me clean." 3 Jesus reached out his hand and touched the man. "I am willing," he said. "Be clean!" Immediately he was cured of his leprosy.	
Matthew 27:51-54 At that moment the curtain of the temple was torn in two from top to bottom. The earth shook, the rocks split 52 and the tombs broke open. The bodies of many holy people who had died were raised to life. 53 They came out of the tombs after Jesus' resurrection and went into the holy city and appeared to many people. 54 When the centurion and those with him who were guarding Jesus saw the earthquake and all that had happened, they were terrified, and exclaimed, "Surely he was the Son of God!"	Divine
Matthew 27:50 And when Jesus had cried out again in a loud voice, he gave up his spirit.	Human

The Resurrection of Christ

1 Corinthians 15:3-22

For what I received I passed on to you as of first importance: that Christ died for our sins according to the Scriptures, 4 that he was buried, that he was raised on the third day according to the Scriptures, 5 and that he appeared to Peter, and then to the Twelve. 6 After that, he appeared to more than five hundred of the brothers at the same time, most of whom are still living, though some have fallen asleep. 7 Then he appeared to James, then to all the apostles, 8 and last of all he appeared to me also, as to one abnormally born.

9 For I am the least of the apostles and do not even deserve to be called an apostle, because I persecuted the church of God.

10 But by the grace of God I am what I am, and his grace to me was not without effect. No, I worked harder than all of them-yet not I, but the grace of God that was with me. 11 Whether, then, it was I or they, this is what we preach, and this is what you believed.

12 But if it is preached that Christ has been raised from the dead, how can some of you say that there is no resurrection of the dead? 13 If there is no resurrection of the dead, then not even Christ has been raised. 14 And if Christ has not been raised, our preaching is useless and so is your faith. 15 More than that, we are then found to be false witnesses about God, for we have testified about God that he raised Christ from the dead. But he did not raise him if in fact the dead are not raised. 16 For if the dead are not raised, then Christ has not been raised either. 17 And if Christ has not been raised, your faith is futile; you are still in your sins. 18 Then those also who have fallen asleep in Christ are lost. 19 If only for this life we have hope in Christ, we are to be pitied more than all men.

20 But Christ has indeed been raised from the dead, the first fruits of those who have fallen asleep. 21 For since death came through a man, the resurrection of the dead comes also through a man. 22 For as in Adam all die, so in Christ all will be made alive.

Why was it not possible for Christ to be held permanently under death, even though he died for our sins?

The death of Jesus the God-Man completely paid and canceled the penalty for sin. Therefore death had lost its claim on him.

What was the difference between Christ's resurrected (glorified body) and his body before he was crucified?

His glorified body is not mortal (able to die) and is not subject to decay, such as sickness and aging.

What event, if it occurred, would disprove Christianity?

Finding the bones of Christ.

> **1 Corinthians 15:14**
> And if Christ has not been raised, our preaching is useless and so is your faith.

Why can we trust the Bible?

It is historical, and the history is verified by independent sources. There are many preserved ancient and historical texts, more than any other ancient document. Many of the very specific prophecies have already been fulfilled.

Here are five truths that are demonstrated by Christ's resurrection:

- He is the Son of God.
- He fully satisfied God's just wrath that was due for the sins of the people.
- He conquered death.
- He conquered Satan, the devil. Gen 3:15.
- He is the Lord of the living and the dead.

The Offices of Christ

WSC 23. How is Christ our redeemer?

As our redeemer, Christ is a prophet, priest, and king in both his humiliation and his exaltation.

Office	Summary	Scriptures
Prophet	Christ reveals the will of God to us for our salvation (WSC 24)	**Matthew 7:28-29** The crowds were amazed at his teaching, 29 because he taught as one who had authority, and not as their teachers of the law.
Priest	Christ offered himself up once as a sacrifice for us to satisfy divine justice and to reconcile us to God, and He continually intercedes for us. (WSC 25)	**Hebrews 9:24-25** For Christ did not enter a man-made sanctuary that was only a copy of the true one; he entered heaven itself, now to appear for us in God's presence. 25 Nor did he enter heaven to offer himself again and again, the way the high priest enters the Most Holy Place every year with blood that is not his own. **Luke 4:16-19** He went to Nazareth, where he had been brought up, and on the Sabbath day he went into the synagogue, as was his custom. And he stood up to read. 17 The scroll of the prophet Isaiah was handed to him. Unrolling it, he found the place where it is written: 18 "The Spirit of the Lord is on me, because he has anointed me to preach good news to the poor. He has sent me to proclaim freedom for the prisoners and recovery of sight for the blind, to release the oppressed, 19 to proclaim the year of the Lord's favor."

King	As a king, Christ brings us under his power, rules and defends us, and restrains and conquers all his and all our enemies. (WSC 26)	**Revelation 19:15** Out of his mouth comes a sharp sword with which to strike down the nations. "He will rule them with an iron scepter." He treads the winepress of the fury of the wrath of God Almighty. 16 On his robe and on his thigh he has this name written: KING OF KINGS AND LORD OF LORDS. **1 Corinthians 15:25-26** For he must reign until he has put all his enemies under his feet. 26 The last enemy to be destroyed is death.

How does Christ execute the office of a prophet today?

Through his written Word, the Bible. By sending his Holy Spirit, who illuminates our hearts and minds so that we can receive and understand the truth revealed in the scriptures.

How does Christ execute the office of a priest today?

Christ continues to make intercession for his people as he ministers at the right hand of God the Father in heaven.

Hebrews 7:25

Therefore he is able to save completely those who come to God through him, because he always lives to intercede for them.

How does Christ execute the office of a king today?

- By restraining and overcoming all the enemies of his people.

- By powerfully ordaining all things to his own glory.

- By judging those who do not know God or obey his gospel.

- By bestowing saving grace upon his people by the work of the Holy Spirit.

- By preserving and supporting his people under all their temptations and sufferings, so that they are never overwhelmed with troubles, but are kept from despair.

Review

Lesson 9 – We learned from WSC 21 that: There is only one redeemer for mankind – Jesus Christ, the eternal Son of God. God chooses those who are redeemed. God the Son became a man – though he was not always a man. Jesus continues to be both man and God to this day and will remain so forever. Jesus has two natures – God and man, yet he is one person.

The names of Jesus tell us much about him: Immanuel (God with us), Jesus (Jehovah saves), Christ (Messiah or Anointed One). There are many other names and titles of Christ throughout the Scriptures. Jesus has two natures: human and divine. Only a man could pay the debt of obedience to the moral law that was owed by man. Only a perfect man without debt to God could pay the ransom. Only God and not a man alone could have sufficient value to redeem the multitude of God's elect.

The resurrection of Christ is the central event in Christianity. It demonstrated that Jesus is the Son of God; he fully satisfied God's wrath due to the sins of the people; he conquered death; he conquered Satan; he is the lord of the living and the dead.

Finally, we learned that Jesus is our prophet, priest, and king. As prophet he reveals the will of God and way of salvation. As priest he offers himself up once to satisfy divine justice and to reconcile us to God. As king he brings us under his power, rules and defends us, and conquers all his and our enemies.

Prayer

- Father – we thank you for Jesus
  - That Jesus became a man to be the only one who could rescue us by living perfectly for us and satisfying the penalty of sin on our behalf
  - That the resurrection of Jesus proves that his sacrifice was accepted and that we are set free
  - That Jesus is God with us, the one who saves his us from our sins
- Jesus – you are our redeemer and our prophet, priest, and king
  - As our prophet he reveals God's will for our salvation
  - As our priest, he sacrificed himself for us and lives to intercede for us
  - As our king, he rules and defends us and restrains and conquers all his and our enemies
- Praise be to God for this great salvation

Lesson 10

Jesus – Justification and Adoption

The Old Testament Clearly Pointed to the Final Work of Christ and our Adoption

Introduction

We are made righteous in God's sight by the work of Christ. The Old Testament sacrificial system was not an alternate path to salvation, but a powerful foreshadowing of what Christ accomplished for all the redeemed from Genesis onward. We are not only declared righteous in Christ, but we are adopted: made to be God's sons and daughters and the brothers and sisters of Christ.

What does the justice of God require as a response to sin?

God's justice requires that sin is punished. The Covenant of Works stipulated that failure to obey God's moral law would result in death and alienation.

Why can God not just forgive and forget?

To simply pardon sin without any penalty for the sin would deny the justice and holiness of God.

What would be bad about a God who merely forgave sin without atonement?

If God merely overlooked sin or forgave it freely it would mean that:

- Sin and wrongdoing would continue without restraint or consequence.

- God would be less than holy and just, because he would tolerate sin.

- We could not count on God to maintain his good will toward us after he had forgiven our sin. If God could deny himself and overlook sin, than what would restrain him from reversing his forgiveness and punishing us? We would lack any real security.

The Old Testament Tabernacle and Sacrificial System

The inner, western room was called the Holy of Holies. It 15 feet square, and it contained only one piece of furniture – the holiest item in the tabernacle, the Ark of the Covenant. The ark was a chest made of acacia wood covered with gold, three feet nine inches long and two foot three inches in width and height. In addition, a gold border extended above the top of the ark to keep the lid stationary. The ark also had golden rings on each side so it could be transported with poles that were placed through the rings. Two gold cherubim faced each other on the Mercy Seat, the lid of the ark. The ark contained a copy of the Ten Commandments written on stone tablets, a copy of the entire law of Moses or the Pentateuch; a gold pot filled with Manna, and Aaron's rod that budded.

The outer, eastern room was called the Holy Place. 15 feet wide and 30 feet long, it was entered through the blue, scarlet, and purple linen curtains which served as a door. This door was always aligned toward the east. The Holy Space contained three items. On its western side, next to the veil, was the altar of incense, or golden altar, made of acacia wood overlaid with gold. The morning and evening incense was burned on this altar. On the northern side of the Holy Place was the seven-branched golden lampstand, or candlestick, comprised of a pedestal, a shaft, and three branches extending to both sides of the shaft. This lampstand was made of fine gold. On the southern side of the Holy Place was the table for the Showbread, or bread of the presence. This table was made of gold-covered acacia wood three feet long, one and a half wide, and two feet three inches high.

Surrounding the main building of the tabernacle was a spacious courtyard 150 feet long in its east-west direction and 75 feet wide from north to south. This courtyard was surrounded by a fence seven and a half feet high, formed of pillars with silverwork, resting in brass sockets, placed seven and a half feet apart, and hung with fine linen. The tabernacle was in the western half of this courtyard. In the eastern half stood the altar of burnt offering. The bronze laver was placed between the altar and the tabernacle. The priests washed themselves at the laver before entering the tabernacle, after they had made the sacrifices at the altar.

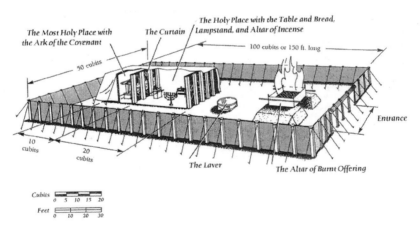

Tabernacle descriptions are from Wikipedia. Drawing from Google Images.

What is so significant about there being an inner room (the Most Holy Place) in the tabernacle?

- Only the High Priest can enter it
- It can only be entered once a year, by God's direction

- The High Priest offers one sacrifice for all the people

Key Elements of the Old Testament Sacrificial System

The penalty for sin is death (shed blood required).

> **Leviticus 17:11-12**
>
> For the life of a creature is in the blood, and I have given it to you to make atonement for yourselves on the altar; it is the blood that makes atonement for one's life.

The high priest must also offer a sacrifice for his own sin and his family's sin.

> **Leviticus 16:11-12**
>
> Aaron shall bring the bull for his own sin offering to make atonement for himself and his household, and he is to slaughter the bull for his own sin offering.

The sacrifice offered must be without blemish.

> **Leviticus 22:17-22**
>
> The LORD said to Moses, 18 "Speak to Aaron and his sons and to all the Israelites and say to them: 'If any of you--either an Israelite or an alien living in Israel--presents a gift for a burnt offering to the LORD, either to fulfill a vow or as a freewill offering, 19 you must present a male without defect from the cattle, sheep or goats in order that it may be accepted on your behalf. 20 Do not bring anything with a defect, because it will not be accepted on your behalf. 21 When anyone brings from the herd or flock a fellowship offering to the LORD to fulfill a special vow or as a freewill offering, it must be without defect or blemish to be acceptable. 22 Do not offer to the LORD the blind, the injured or the maimed, or anything with warts or festering or running sores. Do not place

any of these on the altar as an offering made to the LORD by
fire

The priest makes a sacrifice of blood for the whole people.

Leviticus 16:15-22

He shall then slaughter the goat for the sin offering for the
people and take its blood behind the curtain and do with it as
he did with the bull's blood: He shall sprinkle it on the
atonement cover and in front of it. 16 In this way he will make
atonement for the Most Holy Place because of the uncleanness
and rebellion of the Israelites, whatever their sins have been.

**The sacrifice on the Day of Atonement removed the people's
sins from them.**

Leviticus 16:20

When Aaron has finished making atonement for the Most Holy
Place, the Tent of Meeting and the altar, he shall bring forward
the live goat. 21 He is to lay both hands on the head of the live
goat and confess over it all the wickedness and rebellion of the
Israelites--all their sins--and put them on the goat's head. He
shall send the goat away into the desert in the care of a man
appointed for the task. 22 The goat will carry on itself all their
sins to a solitary place; and the man shall release it in the
desert.

The Limitations of the Old Testament Sacrifices

Hebrews 9:1

Now the first covenant had regulations for worship and also an
earthly sanctuary. 2 A tabernacle was set up. In its first room
were the lampstand, the table and the consecrated bread; this
was called the Holy Place. 3 Behind the second curtain was a

room called the Most Holy Place, 4 which had the golden altar of incense and the gold-covered ark of the covenant. This ark contained the gold jar of manna, Aaron's staff that had budded, and the stone tablets of the covenant. 5 Above the ark were the cherubim of the Glory, overshadowing the atonement cover. But we cannot discuss these things in detail now. 6 When everything had been arranged like this, the priests entered regularly into the outer room to carry on their ministry. 7 But only the high priest entered the inner room, and that only once a year, and never without blood, which he offered for himself and for the sins the people had committed in ignorance. 8 The Holy Spirit was showing by this that the way into the Most Holy Place had not yet been disclosed as long as the first tabernacle was still standing. 9 This is an illustration for the present time, indicating that the gifts and sacrifices being offered were not able to clear the conscience of the worshiper. 10 They are only a matter of food and drink and various ceremonial washings-external regulations applying until the time of the new order.

Pardon was significantly limited under the sacrificial system

- Pardon required a temporary and continual sacrifice.
- Pardon did not change the heart or provide a perfected conscience.
- Fellowship with God was very limited.

Jesus is a Superior Priest, Sacrifice, and Tabernacle

Hebrews 9:11

When Christ came as high priest of the good things that are already here, he went through the greater and more perfect tabernacle that is not man-made, that is to say, not a part of this creation. 12 He did not enter by means of the blood of goats and calves; but he entered the Most Holy Place once for all by his own blood, having obtained eternal redemption. 13 The blood of goats and bulls and the ashes of a heifer sprinkled on those who are ceremonially unclean sanctify them so that they are outwardly clean. 14 How much more, then, will the blood of Christ, who through the eternal Spirit offered himself unblemished to God, cleanse our consciences from acts that lead to death, so that we may serve the living God!

Hebrews 9:24-25

For Christ did not enter a man-made sanctuary that was only a copy of the true one; he entered heaven itself, now to appear for us in God's presence. 25 Nor did he enter heaven to offer himself again and again, the way the high priest enters the Most Holy Place every year with blood that is not his own.

What did the blood of animals slain in the tabernacle courtyard accomplish in the Old Covenant?

It covered guilt, suspended judgment, and pointed to the coming Savior.

What does the blood of Christ accomplish?

It purifies our conscience, writes God's law on our hearts, gives us access to God, and provides full acceptance.

Note the Differences between the Priests of Israel and Christ *the Lord*

Jewish Priests	Christ The High Priest
Perform sacrifices continually, day after day.	Jesus sacrifices once and then sits down.
Priests offer sacrifices that cannot take away sins.	Jesus by one sacrifice makes perfect forever.
Never makes the people holy.	Makes the people holy – sprinkled with blood.

Because of Christ we have full confidence to come to God's throne; a throne of Grace.

Hebrews 4:14-16

Therefore, since we have a great high priest who has gone through the heavens, Jesus the Son of God, let us hold firmly to the faith we profess. 15 For we do not have a high priest who is unable to sympathize with our weaknesses, but we have one who has been tempted in every way, just as we are-yet was without sin. 16 Let us then approach the throne of grace with confidence, so that we may receive mercy and find grace to help us in our time of need.

Hebrews 10:19

Therefore, brothers, since we have confidence to enter the Most Holy Place by the blood of Jesus, 20 by a new and living way opened for us through the curtain, that is, his body, 21 and since we have a great priest over the house of God, 22 let us draw near to God with a sincere heart in full assurance of faith, having our hearts sprinkled to cleanse us from a guilty conscience and having our bodies washed with pure water.

What do we experience when our conscience is purified?

- Assurance of forgiveness
- Assurance of lasting peace with God
- Assurance of being God's loved child

Justification

> **WSC 33. What is justification?**
>
> *Justification is the act of God's grace by which He pardons all our sins and accepts us as righteous in his sight. He does so only because he counts the righteousness of Christ as ours. Justification is received by faith alone.*

Because of the work of Christ our priest, God regards us as totally righteous and we are set free from any obligation or consequence of our guilt?

How do people try to earn justification?

- Trying to be good enough
- Feeling bad or sorry about their sins
- Performing acts that express how sorry they are
- Observing religious duties

All these are attempts to do something or be something to earn God's good will.

Why does this not work?

> **Galatians 2:16**
> A man is not justified by observing the law, but by faith in Jesus Christ. So we, too, have put our faith in Christ Jesus that we may be justified by faith in Christ and not by observing the law, because by observing the law no one will be justified.

We can't be justified by being good (obeying the law): We are sinners in Adam, have sinned already ourselves, and are too sinful to obey in the future.

Justification has been called the great exchange. What has been exchanged?

Christ receives the penalty for our sin in exchange for his righteousness given to us.

He is treated as if he were sinful and in exchange we are treated as if we are righteous.

What do you then contribute to your salvation?

Your sin.

What about your faith – don't you contribute that?

No. God provides our faith as a gift to us.

> **Ephesians 2:8-9**
> For it is by grace you have been saved, through faith-and this not from yourselves, it is the gift of God- 9 not by works, so that no one can boast.

Justification results in our being declared righteous.

Imagine being pardoned by the governor for committing murder. You are freed from the penalty of your crime.

But what is your personal relationship to the judge after being pardoned?

The same as before. You go your separate ways and may never meet again. You are declared "not guilty" by the judge, but you have not had a change of relationship to him.

Adoption

After the judge declares that you are "not guilty" of murder, he does a remarkable thing. He immediately signs papers of adoption and you become his child.

You now have free access to the judge, live at his house, eat at his table, go on vacations, etc.. Do you see the difference between justification and adoption? The incredible thing about what Christ accomplished for us is that we have not only been justified, but we have been adopted.

Jesus calls us family

Hebrews 2:11-12

Both the one who makes men holy and those who are made holy are of the same family. So Jesus is not ashamed to call them brothers. 12 He says, "I will declare your name to my brothers; in the presence of the congregation ..

He chose us in eternity

Ephesians 1:4-7

For he chose us in him before the creation of the world to be holy and blameless in his sight. In love 5 he predestined us to be adopted as his sons through Jesus Christ, in accordance with his pleasure and will- 6 to the praise of his glorious grace, which he has freely given us in the One he loves.

Born by God's decision

John 1:12-13

Yet to all who received him, to those who believed in his name, he gave the right to become children of God- 13 children born not of natural descent, nor of human decision or a husband's will, but born of God.

Romans 8:14-16

Because those who are led by the Spirit of God are sons of God. 15 For you did not receive a spirit that makes you a slave again to fear, but you received the Spirit of sonship. And by him we cry, "Abba, Father."

Heirs of promise

Galatians 3:26-29

You are all sons of God through faith in Christ Jesus, 27 for all of you who were baptized into Christ have clothed yourselves with Christ. 28 There is neither Jew nor Greek, slave nor free, male nor female, for you are all one in Christ Jesus. 29 If you belong to Christ, then you are Abraham's seed, and heirs according to the promise.

Lavished with the Father's love

John 3:1

How great is the love the Father has lavished on us, that we should be called children of God! And that is what we are!

Matthew 6:9

"This, then, is how you should pray: Our Father in heaven, hallowed be your name.....

Justification	Adoption
Change in our legal status	Change in our personal status
Makes us righteous in God's sight	Makes us God's Children
Makes us citizens of God's kingdom	Makes us members of God's family
God pardons us	God gives us his Spirit
God acts as our judge	God acts as our father

Review

Lesson 10 – God's response to sin is to impose a penalty – alienation and death. God cannot merely pardon sin without a payment, for this would deny his holiness and justice. Also, if God merely pardoned sin – we would not be secure in our pardon, as God could deny himself again by reversing his pardon and punishing us.

We examined the Jewish tabernacle and how sacrifices were made in ancient Israel to address the sins of the people. Once a year, on the Day of Atonement, the High Priest would make a sacrifice for all the people in the Most Holy Place. The book of Hebrews describes how all this pointed to the work of our great High Priest – Jesus. Jesus entered the Holy Place in Heaven once to present himself as the sacrifice for his people. This has brought permanent forgiveness, access to God, and a clear conscience.

We studied justification; which is being declared righteous based upon the work of Christ. But, we are not only justified, but adopted! We are made children of the living God and given the Holy Spirit by which we cry "Abba Father", knowing that we love God, are accepted by him, and will dwell with him forever.

<u>Prayer</u>

- Father – we praise you for the incredible work of Jesus, our High Priest, who fulfills all that the Old Testament sacrificial system points to
    - His one sacrifice cleanses us from sin forever
    - His one sacrifice has made our consciences clean
    - His one sacrifice ensure victory over all his and our enemies
    - His one sacrifice makes his people truly holy and righteous
- Father – we thank you father for the assurance that you have given us because of Jesus
    - Assurance of forgiveness
    - Assurance of lasting peace with God
    - Assurance of being God's loved child
    - Assurance that we will spend eternity in your loving presence.

Lesson 11

The Holy Spirit and Effectual Calling

How God Saves his People

Introduction

We have learned that mankind is sinful; marred in every aspect of mind and heart. As fallen people we are alienated from God and do not love and enjoy him as we were created to. So how are we then saved? How can we come to love God and receive what Christ has done for us? The answer is that God saves us from sin and ourselves. He regenerates our dead heart. It is the work of God to make a Christian.

The Work of the Holy Spirit

The Holy Spirit Anoints

Christ means Anointed One. God anoints Jesus for his work at his baptism.

> **John 1:32-34**
> Then John gave this testimony: "I saw the Spirit come down from heaven as a dove and remain on him. 33 I would not have known him, except that the one who sent me to baptize with water told me, 'The man on whom you see the Spirit come down and remain is he who will baptize with the Holy Spirit.' 34 I have seen and I testify that this is the Son of God."

The Holy Spirit gives spiritual birth to men

How are we to enter the kingdom of God? We must be reborn or recreated. This is the work of the Holy Spirit and cannot be predicted (anymore than we can predict the wind).

John 3:5-8

Jesus answered, "I tell you the truth, no one can enter the kingdom of God unless he is born of water and the Spirit. 6 Flesh gives birth to flesh, but the Spirit gives birth to spirit. 7 You should not be surprised at my saying, 'You must be born again.' 8 The wind blows wherever it pleases. You hear its sound, but you cannot tell where it comes from or where it is going. So it is with everyone born of the Spirit."

We worship in and by the Holy Spirit

Just as we must be spiritually born of the Spirit to enter the kingdom, we worship in and by the Holy Spirit.

John 4:22-24

Yet a time is coming and has now come when the true worshipers will worship the Father in spirit and truth, for they are the kind of worshipers the Father seeks. 24 God is spirit, and his worshipers must worship in spirit and in truth."

We are indwelled by the Holy Spirit

We are not only born again by the work of the Holy Spirit, we are also indwelt by the Holy Spirit.

John 7:37-39

On the last and greatest day of the Feast, Jesus stood and said in a loud voice, "If anyone is thirsty, let him come to me and drink. 38 Whoever believes in me, as the Scripture has said, streams of living water will flow from within him." 39 By this he meant the Spirit, whom those who believed in him were later to receive. Up to that time the Spirit had not been given, since Jesus had not yet been glorified.

The Holy Spirit is our Comforter and Counselor

The word comfort actually come from com forte which means "with strength". To bring comfort is to bring strength. This is what the Holy Spirit does. He is always with us and assures us of the good will and presence of God.

John 14:15-18

If you love me, you will obey what I command. 16 And I will ask the Father, and he will give you another Counselor to be with you forever- 17 the Spirit of truth. The world cannot accept him, because it neither sees him nor knows him. But you know him, for he lives with you and will be in you.

The Holy Spirit is our Teacher

The Holy Spirit works within us to remind us of God's Word. One result of this is peace in our hearts.

John 14:25-27

All this I have spoken while still with you. 26 But the Counselor, the Holy Spirit, whom the Father will send in my name, will teach you all things and will remind you of everything I have said to you. 27 Peace I leave with you; my peace I give you. I do not give to you as the world gives. Do not let your hearts be troubled and do not be afraid.

The Holy Spirit Speaks of Christ

The Holy Spirit is the Spirit of truth who speaks about the Way, the Truth, and the Life – Jesus.

> **John 15:26**
>
> When the Counselor comes, whom I will send to you from the Father, the Spirit of truth who goes out from the Father, he will testify about me.
>
> **John 16:12-15**
>
> I have much more to say to you, more than you can now bear. 13 But when he, the Spirit of truth, comes, he will guide you into all truth. He will not speak on his own; he will speak only what he hears, and he will tell you what is yet to come. 14 He will bring glory to me by taking from what is mine and making it known to you. 15 All that belongs to the Father is mine. That is why I said the Spirit will take from what is mine and make it known to you.

The Holy Spirit convicts of Sin

The first thing that happens to a person upon whom the Spirit is working, is that the person starts to experience guilt, followed by an expectation of judgment, and then a turning of the person towards Christ as savior and Lord.

> **John 16:7-9**
>
> But I tell you the truth: It is for your good that I am going away. Unless I go away, the Counselor will not come to you; but if I go, I will send him to you. 8 When he comes, he will convict the world of guilt in regard to sin and righteousness and judgment.

Dead people are unable to seek or come to God

One of the most important things the Holy Spirit does is to cause those who are dead in sins to be saved.

The truth is that we are dead spiritually and unable to come to faith without the Holy Spirit changing our heart. We do not have the love for God that we were meant to have. In our sin we have no desire to enjoy and glorify the true God. We may seek his blessings, but we do not desire God for himself.

Everyone sinful. No one seeks God.

> **Romans 3:10-11**
> There is no one righteous, not even one; 11 there is no one who understands, no one who seeks God.

No place for God

> **Psalm 10:4**
> In his pride the wicked does not seek him; in all his thoughts there is no room for God.

Religious with a dead heart

> **Isaiah 29:13**
> The Lord says: "These people come near to me with their mouth and honor me with their lips, but their hearts are far from me. Their worship of me is made up only of rules taught by men.

Are people spiritually dead and unable to come to God on their own?

Yes. Christian conversion is not the work of people who are somehow more moral, or wise, or intelligent. Everyone is dead in sins and unable to seek God.

But the world is full of religious people who are seeking God. What about them?

To be merely religious is to seek our own benefit. This seeking can be for peace, contentment, acceptance, self-improvement, power, or any other benefit. But it is not seeking the only true God as he is, in order to love, glorify, and enjoy him. God created us to be much more than good people; he created us to be his loving children. The human race lost that ability at the fall of Adam. This is spiritual death and is beyond our own solving.

The Role of the Holy Sprit in Effective (or Effectual) Calling

WSC 29. How do we then take part in the redemption Christ brought?

We take part in the redemption Christ bought when the Holy Spirit effectively applies it to us.

We were dead and then made alive by God

Ephesians 2:1-5

As for you, you were dead in your transgressions and sins, 2 in which you used to live when you followed the ways of this world and of the ruler of the kingdom of the air, the spirit who is now at work in those who are disobedient. 3 All of us also lived among them at one time, gratifying the cravings of our sinful nature and following its desires and thoughts. Like the rest, we were by nature objects of wrath. 4 But because of his great love for us, God, who is rich in mercy, 5 made us alive with Christ even when we were dead in transgressions-it is by grace you have been saved.

Called according to God's purpose

Romans 8:28

To them who are the called according to his purpose.

The Holy Spirit effectively applies redemption to us. What does this mean?

It means that the Holy Spirit is powerful enough to make redemption happen even though we are enemies of God and don't seek him.

WSC 30. How does the Holy Spirit work to apply redemption to us?

The Spirit applies to us the redemption Christ bought by producing faith in us and so uniting us to Christ in our effective calling.

The Holy Spirit produces faith in us.

The Holy Spirit unites us to Christ in his death and resurrection.

Where did your faith come from?

> *This is the bottom line: we would no more come to faith without the miracle work of the Holy Spirit than a dead man could climb out of his casket. Faith is given to us. It is not what we give to God.*

Ephesians 2:8-10
For it is by grace you have been saved, through faith-and this not from yourselves, it is the gift of God- 9 not by works, so that no one can boast.

WSC 31. What is effective calling?

Effective calling is the work of God's Spirit, Who convinces us that we are sinful and miserable, Who enlightens our minds in the knowledge of Christ, and Who renews our wills. This is how He persuades and makes us able to receive Jesus Christ, who is freely offered to us in the Gospel.

- The result of effective calling is Salvation
- The Holy Spirit convinces us that we are sinful and miserable
- The Holy Spirit enlightens our minds so we know that Christ is Lord and Savior
- The Holy Spirit transforms our hearts to embrace Christ.

- The Holy Spirit persuades us and makes us able to receive Jesus Christ
- The Holy Spirit causes us to be reborn, with new life and affection for God (John 3)

How much power does this effective calling take?

The power of bringing new life to us is like the power of Christ's resurrection.

Made alive by God's mighty strength

Ephesians 1:18-23

I pray also that the eyes of your heart may be enlightened in order that you may know the hope to which he has called you, the riches of his glorious inheritance in the saints, 19 and his incomparably great power for us who believe. That power is like the working of his mighty strength, 20 which he exerted in Christ when he raised him from the dead and seated him at his right hand in the heavenly realms, 21 far above all rule and authority, power and dominion, and every title that can be given, not only in the present age but also in the one to come. 22 And God placed all things under his feet and appointed him to be head over everything for the church, 23 which is his body, the fullness of him who fills everything in every way.

The human response to the Gospel aside from the miracle work of effective calling:

1 Corinthians 1:22-25

Jews demand miraculous signs and Greeks look for wisdom, 23 but we preach Christ crucified: a stumbling block to Jews and foolishness to Gentiles, 24 but to those whom God has called, both Jews and Greeks, Christ the power of God and the wisdom of God. 25 For the foolishness of God is wiser than man's wisdom, and the weakness of God is stronger than man's strength.

- Atheists deny God.
- The religious non-Christian denies Christ and his work.
- The moralistic "Christian" depends on their goodness rather than Christ's work.

Who	Attitude	The Gospel is
Religious	Show me how I can earn my standing before God.	A stumbling block – "I'm fine. I don't need a savior."
Pagan	Christ is not God. Or: There is no God.	A fairy tale – foolish
The Called	I am sinful, Christ – you are my only hope, save me by your work.	The power of God and the Wisdom of God

Review

Lesson 11– First we learned about the Holy Spirit and his role by walking through the gospel of John. We learned that: the Holy Spirit:

- Anointed Jesus for his ministry
- Convicts men of sin and points to Christ as Savior
- Gives spiritual birth to men
- Indwells God's people and guides them in true worship
- Is our Comforter and Counselor and Teacher

One of the most important things the Holy Spirit does is to cause those who are dead in sins to be saved. The truth is that we are dead spiritually and unable to come to faith without the Holy Spirit changing our heart. We take part in the redemption Christ bought when the Holy Spirit effectively applies it to us. The Spirit applies to us the redemption Christ bought by producing faith in us and so uniting us to Christ in our effective calling. Why are we saved? Because the Holy Spirit effectively applies the work of Christ to us.

Where did your faith come from? This is the bottom line: we would no more come to faith without the miracle work of the Holy Spirit than a dead man could climb out of his casket. Faith is given to us. It is not what we give to God. The result of effective calling is Salvation: The Holy Spirit convinces us that we are sinful and miserable. He enlightens our minds that Christ is Lord and Savior, and he transforms our hearts to embrace Christ.

Prayer

- Father – thank you for the work of the Holy Spirit:
    - Who Anointed Jesus for his ministry
    - Who convicts men of Sin and points to Christ as Savior
    - Who gives spiritual birth to men
    - Who indwells God's people and guides them in true worship
    - Who is our Comforter and Counselor and Teacher
- Father – thank you for calling us to yourself and overcoming our rebellion.
    - You did for us what we could not do for ourselves.
    - You created faith in us
    - You gave us a new heart
    - You have made us your children forevermore

Lesson 12

The Holy Spirit – Regeneration and Conversion

A New Life in Christ

Introduction

What happens when the Holy Spirit effectively calls us? Does God only regard us as forgiven and righteous or is there an actual change in us? If we were formerly dead to God, how are we now alive to him? In this lesson we examine two results of effectual calling: regeneration and conversion.

Regeneration

WSC 31. What is effective calling?

Effective calling is the work of God's Spirit, Who convinces us that we are sinful and miserable, Who enlightens our minds in the knowledge of Christ, and Who renews our wills. This is how He persuades and makes us able to receive Jesus Christ, who is freely offered to us in the Gospel.

The Holy Spirit's causes us to be regenerated.

Regeneration: a definition

Re – Again   Generate – to give life

Regeneration: To give life again

What is regeneration?

It is that work of the Spirit whereby He implants the new life of Christ in the heart of the sinner.

Formerly Dead

Ephesians 2:1
For you, you were dead in your transgressions and sins,

Given a new living heart

Ezekiel 36:26-27
I will give you a new heart and put a new spirit in you; I will remove from you your heart of stone and give you a heart of flesh. 27 And I will put my Spirit in you and move you to follow my decrees and be careful to keep my laws.

Born of the Spirit

John 3:88
The wind blows wherever it pleases. You hear its sound, but you cannot tell where it comes from or where it is going. So it is with everyone born of the Spirit."

Born into a living and permanent hope

1 Peter 1:3-4
Praise be to the God and Father of our Lord Jesus Christ! In his great mercy he has given us new birth into a living hope through the resurrection of Jesus Christ from the dead, 4 and into an inheritance that can never perish, spoil or fade-kept in heaven for you

How do we enter God's kingdom and his presence? How do we obtain heaven? By doing good works? By making a good choice?

Jesus says that it is not by who we are or what we do, but by the work of God himself.

The story of Nicodemus:

John 3:1-8

Now there was a man of the Pharisees named Nicodemus, a member of the Jewish ruling council. 2 He came to Jesus at night and said, "Rabbi, we know you are a teacher who has come from God. For no one could perform the miraculous signs you are doing if God were not with him." 3 In reply Jesus declared, "I tell you the truth, no one can see the kingdom of God unless he is born again."

4 "How can a man be born when he is old?" Nicodemus asked. "Surely he cannot enter a second time into his mother's womb to be born!" 5 Jesus answered, "I tell you the truth, no one can enter the kingdom of God unless he is born of water and the Spirit. 6 Flesh gives birth to flesh, but the Spirit gives birth to spirit. 7 You should not be surprised at my saying, 'You must be born again.' 8 The wind blows wherever it pleases. You hear its sound, but you cannot tell where it comes from or where it is going. So it is with everyone born of the Spirit."

John 1:10-13

He was in the world, and though the world was made through him, the world did not recognize him. 11 He came to that which was his own, but his own did not receive him. 12 Yet to all who received him, to those who believed in his name, he gave the right to become children of God- 13 children born not of natural descent, nor of human decision or a husband's will, but born of God.

What comes first, regeneration (new life) or faith?

Regeneration comes first.

Why?

Spiritually dead people can't have faith.

What are the steps in the order of salvation?

The steps are: regeneration, faith, justification, sanctification, preservation, and glorification.

How is this salvation accomplished in the elect sinner?

Christ, who is the fullness of our salvation, accomplishes it completely by his Holy Spirit.

Titus 3:5
He saved us, not because of righteous things we had done, but because of his mercy. He saved us through the washing of rebirth and renewal by the Holy Spirit,

What is the first work of the Holy Spirit in the heart of the elect sinner?

The work of regeneration:

John 3:3
In reply Jesus declared, "I tell you the truth, no one can see the kingdom of God unless he is born again."

Does the sinner cooperate in his own regeneration?

Not at all; it is the work of the Holy Spirit, alone. He changes our heart that is dead to God into a heart that is alive to God.

> **Acts 16:14-15**
> One of those listening was a woman named Lydia, a dealer in purple cloth from the city of Thyatira, who was a worshiper of God. The Lord opened her heart to respond to Paul's message.

Conversion

What is conversion?

It is the mortification of the old man of sin and the quickening of the new man in Christ whereby a sinner turns from his wicked way and towards God.

What are the fruits of conversion?

The fruits of conversion are a thankful walk of obedience to God, as we are thankful for the salvation which is ours through faith in Christ.

> **2 Corinthians 7:10**
> Godly sorrow brings repentance that leads to salvation and leaves no regret, but worldly sorrow brings death.

WSC 85. What does God require of us to escape his wrath and the curse, which we deserve?

To escape God's anger and curse, which we deserve for our sin, God requires from us faith in Jesus Christ and repentance unto life along with diligent involvement in all the external ways Christ uses to bring us the benefits of redemption.

What are the two parts of conversion?

- Faith in Jesus Christ

- Repentance unto Life accompanied by attention to the means of grace (worship, fellowship, attention to scripture, prayer, and the sacraments: Baptism and the Lord's Supper)

WSC 86. What is faith in Jesus Christ?

Faith in Jesus Christ is a saving grace, by which we receive and rest on him alone for salvation, as He is offered to us in the gospel.

The first part of conversion is Faith: Turning to Christ.

There are three components of saving faith: knowledge, assent, and trust.

1. Knowledge of the claims of our own sinfulness and the claims of Christ and the Gospel

2. Assent that we are indeed sinners in need of salvation and that Christ is Lord and Savior and the Gospel offer is true

3. Trust in Christ as our only Hope, turn to him for salvation and honor and obey him.

Can Christ save you by being your example for living?

No. Trusting in Christ as your savior saves you; he lived the life you should have lived and died the death you should have died.

To trust in Christ simply as a moral teacher or example is not saving faith.

Again, where can you get this faith?

Faith is a miraculous work of the Holy Spirit who generates new life in us through the gospel being declared to us. The source of faith is not our own disposition, intelligence, goodness, or any other thing about us. It is God's gift to us.

If we can do nothing to gain faith, what do we tell the unbeliever?

We tell them to repent of their sins, believe in Christ, and confess him as Lord and Savior. If they do so, they can be fully assured that God will save them. This is the Gospel!

So, even though we know that the faith to believe is a gift of God, we still call everyone to repent and to believe, realizing that God is at work through the proclamation of the Gospel – bringing people to faith!

Romans 10:9-11

That if you confess with your mouth, "Jesus is Lord," and believe in your heart that God raised him from the dead, you will be saved. 10 For it is with your heart that you believe and are justified, and it is with your mouth that you confess and are saved. 11 As the Scripture says, "Anyone who trusts in him will never be put to shame."

The second part of conversion is Repentance Unto Life

What is repentance?

Turning from sin

Why must we turn from our sin to turn to Christ?

Christ is the only Savior. He delivers us from the wages of sin. We turn to Christ as our Holy God and master and seek to honor and glorify him.

Do Christians need to repent too?

Yes. Even though we have been converted, we still sin. We need to continually and immediately confess our sins. Because of Christ, God is faithful and just to forgive us and cleanse us. Thanks be to God.

WSC 87. What is repentance unto life?

Repentance unto life is a saving grace, by which a sinner, being truly aware of his sinfulness. understands the mercy of God in Christ, grieves for and hates his sins, and turns from them to God, fully intending and striving for a new obedience.

Repentance unto life is a saving grace, by which a sinner:

1. Becomes truly aware of his sinfulness

2. Understands the mercy of God in Christ

3. Grieves for and hates his sin

4. Turns from his sin to God – fully intending and striving for new obedience

Repentance is commanded of all people

Matthew 3:1-2

In those days John the Baptist came, preaching in the Desert of Judea 2 and saying, "Repent, for the kingdom of heaven is near."

Matthew 4:17

From that time on Jesus began to preach, "Repent, for the kingdom of heaven is near."

Mark 6:12-13

They [the disciples] went out and preached that people should repent. 13 They drove out many demons and anointed many sick people with oil and healed them.

Acts 2:38-39

Peter replied, "Repent and be baptized, every one of you, in the name of Jesus Christ for the forgiveness of your sins. And you will receive the gift of the Holy Spirit. 39 The promise is for you and your children and for all who are far off-for all whom the Lord our God will call."

Acts 26:19-21

First to those in Damascus, then to those in Jerusalem and in all Judea, and to the Gentiles also, I [Paul] preached that they should repent and turn to God and prove their repentance by their deeds. 21 That is why the Jews seized me in the temple courts and tried to kill me.

> **1 John 1:8-9**
>
> If we claim to be without sin, we deceive ourselves and the truth is not in us. 9 If we confess our sins, he is faithful and just and will forgive us our sins and purify us from all unrighteousness.

Review

Lesson 12 – We studied the work of the Holy Spirit in our regeneration. Regeneration means to give life again. Regeneration is what the Holy Spirit does in us and for us at our conversion – he persuades us and makes us able to receive Jesus Christ. It took heart surgery to remove our heart of stone, enable us to place our trust in Christ, and give us spiritual life. We see this in John 3 with the story of Nicodemus. Nicodemus, a Pharisee was seeking wisdom for living that would enable him to better please God. Jesus tells Nicodemus that the secret to entering the kingdom of God was to be born again of the Spirit. This birth is not because of who we are or what we decide, but by the work of God that no one can predict.

We talked about Christian conversion. This is not deciding to be a Christian or to join a church. Again, it is the work of God in our life where we turn from our sin and put our faith in Christ and his work. Faith is the gift of God where we receive and rest on Christ alone for salvation, as he is freely offered to us in the gospel. As we turn to Christ we also turn from sin, hating it and intending and striving for a new obedience.

These steps in conversion are a result of the Holy Spirit working through the presented gospel:

- A sinner becomes truly aware of his sinfulness and,
- Understands the mercy of God in Christ and,
- Grieves for and hates his sin and,
- Turns from his sin to faith in Christ – fully intending and striving for new obedience.

Prayer

- Father – you are truly both the author and the finisher of the Christian's salvation
    - You bring the gospel to us while we are dead
    - You give us a new and living heart
    - You bring us alive by the Spirit
    - You create saving faith in us
    - You cause us to repent; we turn from sin and turn to Christ
    - You give us a living and permanent hope
    - You forgive us and cleanse us from unrighteousness as we confess our sins
- Father – we pray for those who do not believe upon you, asking that your Gospel would come to them in the power of the Holy Spirit – that they might be convinced of their sin, and convinced of the work of the Savior, and place their trust in him alone for their salvation.

Lesson 13

The Holy Spirit – Sanctification and Assurance

Secure in the Family of God and Becoming More Like Christ

Introduction

God saves us by his effective calling – which results in our being born again (regeneration), faith, and being united to Christ. To do this the Holy Spirit convinces us that we are sinful and miserable, enlightens our minds in the knowledge of Christ, and renews our wills. But the Holy Spirit's work does not end with our regeneration and conversion. His work continues in us to renew us. We become increasingly dead to sin and alive to Christ.

The Benefits of Being Called

WSC 32. What are the benefits that come in this life to those who are effectually called?

In this life those who are effectively called share justification, adoption, sanctification, and the other benefits that either go with or come from them.

- Justification (declared righteous)

- Adoption (becoming a child of God with all its rights)

- Sanctification (made new and increasingly dead to sin and alive to righteousness)

At the Time of Salvation – God Acts

By the <u>act</u> of God the following happens simultaneously at the moment of conversion:

- Regeneration
  (made alive to God)

- Faith
  (trust in Christ alone for salvation)

- Conversion
  (turning from sin and to Christ)

- Justification
  (pardoned from sin and accepted as righteous)

- Adoption
  (become God's child with all the rights and privileges of being his)

All of these are the results of the powerful effective (or effectual) calling of the Holy Spirit, which brings us the benefits of the saving work of Christ.

We use the single term "salvation" or "justification" to describe all five aspects of becoming a Christian. But all five elements are present.

It is important to understand that this event in all its aspects is an act of God; a completed work at an instant of time. It happens once and never changes.

Sanctification

What does the word sanctification mean?

Let's look at the dictionary definition of Sanctification:

Sanctification is from the Latin word Latin **sanctus** or sacred:

- to set apart to a sacred purpose or to Consecrate

- to free from sin : purify

- to impart or impute sacredness, inviolability, or respect

- to make productive of holiness or piety

Sanctification is a work of God that commences at the time of salvation and continues throughout our lifetime until the moment of death. As a Christian you have not only been pardoned, you have also received new spiritual life. You are a new Child of God. Just as a parent raises a child to maturity, God raises us up to maturity. Just as you are now righteous in Christ – God also plans for you to mature into the very likeness of Christ.

You will one day be a mature child of God – sinless and fully reflecting his image!

WSC 35. What is sanctification?

Sanctification is the work of God's free grace by which our whole person is made new in the image of God, and we are made more and more able to become dead to sin and alive to righteousness.

Because of the fall the image of God in man was shattered and distorted. The work of redemption initiates the work of God in our lives to restore that original and complete image.

Notice that unlike justification and adoption, sanctification is a work rather than an act. It is a life long process – sanctification starts at the moment of our regeneration and is not completed until the moment of death when we enter glory.

At the moment of regeneration we become a new creation and are made increasingly able to become dead to sin and alive to righteousness.

2 Corinthians 5:17
Therefore, if anyone is in Christ, he is a new creation; the old has gone, the new has come!

Do we have a responsibility in becoming mature or do we just sit back and watch God change us?

The Scriptures consistently instruct us to be disciplined in our obedience – to work hard. We need to be faithful to God. We have no option to just sit back. The Christian life is not passive. Why? Because we are new creations, who love God.

---

2 Timothy 2:15-16

Do your best to present yourself to God as one approved, a workman who does not need to be ashamed and who correctly handles the word of truth.

At the same time God is at work. He is faithful to complete his work of sanctification in us. God is at work! He will conform us (shape us) to be like Christ!

Romans 8:28-30

And we know that in all things God works for the good of those who love him, who have been called according to his purpose. 29 For those God foreknew he also predestined to be conformed to the likeness of his Son, that he might be the firstborn among many brothers. 30 And those he predestined, he also called; those he called, he also justified; those he justified, he also glorified.

Paul describes how we are to work hard to work out (make visible and tangible) our salvation as God works in us both to desire and to behave like God's child.

Philippians 2:12-13

Therefore, my dear friends, as you have always obeyed-not only in my presence, but now much more in my absence-continue to work out your salvation with fear and trembling, 13 for it is God who works in you to will and to act according to his good purpose.

Some might say: "If God has forgiven all our sins in Christ and there is no penalty for our sins, hey – we sin all we want!" What do you think about this statement?

> *That is ridiculous way to think. We are not simply forgiven; we are also adopted and given a new heart of love for God. To sin willfully is to deny our new identity.*

Dying to sin and rising with Christ:

Romans 6:1-14

What shall we say, then? Shall we go on sinning so that grace may increase? 2 By no means! We died to sin; how can we live in it any longer? 3 Or don't you know that all of us who were baptized into Christ Jesus were baptized into his death? 4 We were therefore buried with him through baptism into death in order that, just as Christ was raised from the dead through the glory of the Father, we too may live a new life.

5 If we have been united with him like this in his death, we will certainly also be united with him in his resurrection. 6 For we know that our old self was crucified with him so that the body of sin might be done away with, that we should no longer be slaves to sin- 7 because anyone who has died has been freed from sin.

8 Now if we died with Christ, we believe that we will also live with him. 9 For we know that since Christ was raised from the dead, he cannot die again; death no longer has mastery over him. 10 The death he died, he died to sin once for all; but the life he lives, he lives to God.

11 In the same way, count yourselves dead to sin but alive to God in Christ Jesus. 12 Therefore do not let sin reign in your

> mortal body so that you obey its evil desires. 13 Do not offer the parts of your body to sin, as instruments of wickedness, but rather offer yourselves to God, as those who have been brought from death to life; and offer the parts of your body to him as instruments of righteousness. 14 For sin shall not be your master, because you are not under law, but under grace.

What is Paul saying here about this idea that we can now sin freely?

No way. You are crazy to think like that.

What does Paul say we have died to?

As a Christian we have not just died to the penalty of sin – but to sin itself (vs 2)

What two things are parts of our baptism into Christ?

- We are united with Christ in his death (vs 3) – hence the penalty of death for our sins is paid by Jesus

- But we also are united to Christ in his resurrection (vs 4) – raised to new life

- These two - dying and rising are both parts of the work of Christ – they cannot be separated (vs 5)

What happens because our old self is crucified with Christ?

- We are no longer slaves to sin (vs 6)

- Once the penalty has been paid – sin and death have no claim on us (vs 7)

What kind of life have we been raised to?

- A life with Christ (vs 8)

- A life without death forevermore (vs 9)

- A life that is lived for God (vs 10)

So how should we then live?

- We count (consider) ourselves as dead to sin and alive to God (vs 11).

- We no longer let sin reign in us or obey its pull (vs 12).

- We do not use our bodies as instruments (tools) of sin any longer, but tools of righteousness (vs 13),

- Sin is no longer our master, because we are not under law (a slave), but under grace (a child of God!).

Ephesians 4:17-32

So I tell you this, and insist on it in the Lord, that you must no longer live as the Gentiles do, in the futility of their thinking. 18 They are darkened in their understanding and separated from the life of God because of the ignorance that is in them due to the hardening of their hearts. 19 Having lost all sensitivity, they have given themselves over to sensuality so as to indulge in every kind of impurity, with a continual lust for more.

20 You, however, did not come to know Christ that way. 21 Surely you heard of him and were taught in him in accordance with the truth that is in Jesus. 22 You were taught, with regard to your former way of life, to put off your old self, which is being corrupted by its deceitful desires; 23 to be made new in the attitude of your minds; 24 and to put on the new self, created to be like God in true righteousness and holiness.

25 Therefore each of you must put off falsehood and speak truthfully to his neighbor, for we are all members of one body. 26 "In your anger do not sin": Do not let the sun go down while you are still angry, 27 and do not give the devil a foothold. 28 He who has been stealing must steal no longer,

but must work, <u>doing something useful</u> with his own hands, that he may have something to share with those in need.

29 Do not let any unwholesome talk come out of your mouths, but only what is helpful for building others up according to their needs, that it <u>may benefit those who listen</u>. 30 And do not grieve the Holy Spirit of God, with whom you were sealed for the day of redemption. 31 Get rid of all bitterness, rage and anger, brawling and slander, along with every form of malice. 32 Be kind and compassionate to one another, forgiving each other, just as in Christ God forgave you.

How we are not to live as the non-Christian lives:

- Futile thinking
- Darkened understanding
- Separated from God
- Insensitive
- Given over to pleasure and desire for more and more

We are to <u>put off</u> the old ways of corruption and <u>put on</u> the new ways of being like God:

- Put off lying and put on speaking truthfully
- Put off unrighteous anger and the foothold it gives the devil in our life
- Put off stealing and put on useful work
- Put off unwholesome talk and put on speech that honors God
- Put off bitterness, rage, anger, fighting, and evil talk. Put on compassion and forgiveness to others just as Christ does for us.

Assurance

> **WSC 36: What are the four benefits that come from our justification, adoption, and sanctification?**
>
> *The benefits that in this life go with or come from justification, adoption, and sanctification are: the assurance of God's love, peace of conscience, joy in the Holy Spirit, and growing and persevering in grace to the end of our lives.*

What does assurance mean?

Assurance is being certain that we are in Christ – forgiven and adopted.

How can we have this assurance?

By knowing that the gospel is true and that God will do as he says, and that we trust in the work of Christ alone.

Romans 10:9-11

That if you confess with your mouth, "Jesus is Lord," and believe in your heart that God raised him from the dead, you will be saved. 10 For it is with your heart that you believe and are justified, and it is with your mouth that you confess and are saved. 11 As the Scripture says, "Anyone who trusts in him will never be put to shame."

Romans 8:38-39

For I am convinced that neither death nor life, neither angels nor demons, neither the present nor the future, nor any powers, 39 neither height nor depth, nor anything else in all creation, will be able to separate us from the love of God that is in Christ Jesus our Lord.

By seeing one of the fruits of salvation in our life - obedience

> **1 John 2:3-6**
> We know that we have come to know him if we obey his commands. 4 The man who says, "I know him," but does not do what he commands is a liar, and the truth is not in him. 5 But if anyone obeys his word, God's love is truly made complete in him. This is how we know we are in him: 6 Whoever claims to live in him must walk as Jesus did.

Because of the love we have for other Christians

> **1 John 3:14-15**
> We know that we have passed from death to life, because we love our brothers. Anyone who does not love remains in death. 15 Anyone who hates his brother is a murderer, and you know that no murderer has eternal life in him.

Because of the work of the Holy Spirit within us

> **1 John 4:13**
> We know that we live in him and he in us, because he has given us of his Spirit

Because we acknowledge that Jesus is God

> **1 John 4:15**
> If anyone acknowledges that Jesus is the Son of God, God lives in him and he in God.

Because we do not keep sinning all the time

> **1 John 5:18-19**
> We know that anyone born of God does not continue to sin; the one who was born of God keeps him safe, and the evil one cannot harm him.

What can happen to you as a Christian if you become unrepentant to God?

> *Sin and lack of repentance leads to a loss of assurance, peace, and joy (WSC 36). God will discipline you in order to bring you back to right fellowship with him. But if we confess he restores us (1 John 1:9).*

Review

Lesson 13 – We discussed the three benefits that in this life result from our being effectively called by God: Justification, Adoption, and Sanctification. The first two are acts of God, which happen immediately at the time of our conversion. Sanctification, on the other hand, is a work of God that occurs over our lifetime and is not completed until the moment of our death.

Baptism shows us clearly that we both died and arose in Christ. We died to sin and its ways and arose with our Lord to a new life of righteousness as God's child. Hence, it is ridiculous for a Christian to continue to sin as a way of life. We are clearly commanded in Scripture to work hard before God, to please and honor him. We are to put off the old ways of death and estrangement and put on the new ways of righteousness and life. This includes the use of our tongue, all of our talents, our time, and our passions.

The benefits that come from our justification, adoption, and sanctification include our assurance of God's love, a peace of conscience, joy in the Holy Spirit, and growing and persevering in grace. Assurance comes from: proclaiming the gospel as true, by the presence of the Holy Spirit, obedience, fellowship, service, and all the means of grace.

If we lack repentance this leads to lost assurance, a lack of joy, and a lack of persevering in grace. If we find ourselves in this state, we are called to repent to the God who promises to restore us.

Prayer

- Father – thank you that you have provided for our justification, adoption, and sanctification
  - You have united us to Christ in his death
  - You have raised us to new life with Christ
  - You have released us from slavery to sin, and are at work within us to conform us to the image of Jesus
  - You make us able to count ourselves dead to sin and alive to righteousness
  - You enable us to more and more put off the old ways of death and to put on truth, love, compassion, and forgiveness
- Father – thank you for the assurance that we are yours
  - By trusting in the complete work of Christ
  - By seeing the fruit of the Spirit in our lives
  - By the testimony of the love and joy you have placed within us
  - By the gift of repentance and restoration when we sin

Lesson 14

The Future

Our Glorious Destiny

Introduction

So far we have looked at the work of Christ in our salvation and the how the effectual calling of the Holy Spirit results in our regeneration, faith, conversion, justification, adoption, and the work of sanctification. Now, we discuss our destiny as Christians to be fully conformed to the likeness of Christ, to have the effects of the fall fully reversed, and to live in sinless joy. This will be glorious. Hence, a major topic of this lesson is Glorification.

Glorification

A definition of Glorification

Becoming perfect sons and daughters of God

When will glorification happen?

When Jesus comes back

Let's look together at what is called the chain of redemption. Paul talks about the purpose of God in our salvation and each step we experience.

> **Romans 8:28-30**
>
> And we know that in all things God works for the good of those who love him, who have been called according to his purpose. 29 For those God foreknew he also predestined to <u>be</u> <u>conformed to the likeness of his Son</u>, that he might be the firstborn among many brothers. 30 And those he predestined,

> he also called; those he called, he also justified; those he justified, he also glorified.

From this text – what is God's purpose for us?

To be conformed to the likeness of his Son, Jesus.

How does this relate to the chief end of man (WSC 1)?

As we learned the chief end or purpose of man is to glorify God and to enjoy him forever. God through his plan of redeeming us is making that purpose come about. We are redeemed and adopted children of God who will enjoy God forever and honor him as Father for eternity.

To Die is Gain

What is the condition of believers after their death?

After a Christian dies they are consciously in the presence of God, blessed, holy, and awaiting the completion of their redemption by the resurrection of their bodies. This is the state of every believer who has lived and died up to the present time.

WSC 37. What benefits do believers receive from Christ when they die?

When believers die, their souls are made perfectly holy and immediately pass into glory. Their bodies, which are still united to Christ, rest in the grave until the resurrection.

Think of this – death truly has lost its sting for the Christian; death is the occasion of glory.

Don't some people believe we are unconscious after death?

Yes. Some say the soul is asleep after death: we are completely unconscious until the resurrection of our bodies.

How can we know we are conscious after death?

Following are two passages of Scripture that indicate we will be conscious between death and resurrection.

The rich man and Lazarus

Luke 16:22-24

The time came when the beggar died and the angels carried him to Abraham's side. The rich man also died and was buried. 23 In hell, where he was in torment, he looked up and saw Abraham far away, with Lazarus by his side. 24 So he called to him, 'Father Abraham, have pity on me and send Lazarus to dip the tip of his finger in water and cool my tongue, because I am in agony in this fire.'

The man on the cross who believed

Luke 23:43

Jesus answered him, "I tell you the truth, today you will be with me in paradise."

Paul was in prison and writing a letter to the church in Philippi. He was facing the possibility of execution. Imagine the fear in that situation. Yet Paul had courage, knowing that the death sentence will bring him into his Lord's presence.

Phil 1:18-23

Yes, and I will continue to rejoice, 19 for I know that through your prayers and the help given by the Spirit of Jesus Christ, what has happened to me will turn out for my deliverance. 20 I eagerly expect and hope that I will in no way be ashamed, but will have sufficient courage so that now as always Christ will be exalted in my body, whether by life or by death. 21 For to me, to live is Christ and to die is gain. 22 If I am to go on living in the body, this will mean fruitful labor for me. Yet what shall I choose? I do not know! 23 I am torn between the

> two: I desire to depart and be with Christ, which is better by
> far;

Some day we will each face death (unless Jesus returns first).

**Our confidence in glorification makes a huge difference as
we face death. It also brings confidence and purpose as we
face our earthly trials.**

---

2 Cor 5:6-10

Therefore we are always confident and know that as long as we
are at home in the body we are away from the Lord. 7 We live
by faith, not by sight. 8 We are confident, I say, and would
prefer to be away from the body and at home with the Lord. 9
So we make it our goal to please him, whether we are at home
in the body or away from it.

***What does it mean that the bodies of believers are still united
to Christ?***

> *Jesus regards the human bodies of his people, even though
> dead and buried, as something exceedingly precious,
> because he intends to raise them up again at the time of his
> second coming.*

Jesus' Return – The Day of the Lord

So we wait eagerly for the day of Christ's return - the day every
Christian will be glorified. Those dead will be re-united with
their bodies, now glorified. Those alive will be glorified and
their bodies made new instantly.

On that dat Christ will return in glory. 2000 years ago the
angels comforted the disciples by looking to Christ's certain
return.

> **Acts 1:9-11**
>
> After he said this, he was taken up before their very eyes, and a cloud hid him from their sight. 10 They were looking intently up into the sky as he was going, when suddenly two men dressed in white stood beside them. 11 "Men of Galilee," they said, "why do you stand here looking into the sky? This same Jesus, who has been taken from you into heaven, will come back in the same way you have seen him go into heaven."

What is the meaning of the expression "the Last Day"?

The day of the second coming of Christ.

When will that Day be?

> **1 Thessalonians 5:1-3**
>
> Now, brothers, about times and dates we do not need to write to you, 2 for you know very well that the day of the Lord will come like a thief in the night. 3 While people are saying, "Peace and safety," destruction will come on them suddenly, as labor pains on a pregnant woman, and they will not escape.

Many people spend a lot of time trying to predict when Christ will return. Everyone has been wrong so far. The Bible says that the time of his return will be sudden and surprising, like a burglar breaking into your home in the middle of the night or a woman going suddenly into labor.

On that Day - Resurrection of all

The Thessalonians were discouraged at the deaths of their fellow believers. Paul comforts them with these words about the Lord coming again:

> **1 Thessalonians 4:13-18**
>
> Brothers, we do not want you to be ignorant about those who fall asleep, or to grieve like the rest of men, who have no hope. 14 We believe that Jesus died and rose again and so we believe

that God will bring with Jesus those who have fallen asleep in him. 15 According to the Lord's own word, we tell you that we who are still alive, who are left till the coming of the Lord, will certainly not precede those who have fallen asleep. 16 For the Lord himself will come down from heaven, with a loud command, with the voice of the archangel and with the trumpet call of God, and the dead in Christ will rise first. 17 After that, we who are still alive and are left will be caught up together with them in the clouds to meet the Lord in the air. And so we will be with the Lord forever. 18 Therefore encourage each other with these words.

That day will be a day of overwhelming gladness and joy for all Christians. We will be united with Jesus for all eternity.

Who will be resurrected on that day? Christians only?

John 5:25-30

I tell you the truth, a time is coming and has now come when the dead will hear the voice of the Son of God and those who hear will live. 26 For as the Father has life in himself, so he has granted the Son to have life in himself. 27 And he has given him authority to judge because he is the Son of Man.

28 "Do not be amazed at this, for a time is coming when all who are in their graves will hear his voice 29 and come out- those who have done good will rise to live, and those who have done evil will rise to be condemned.

Some believe in two resurrections a thousand years apart. This passage teaches a single resurrection day.

On that Day – Risen like our Lord

> **1 Corinthians 15:20-27**
>
> But Christ has indeed been raised from the dead, the firstfruits of those who have fallen asleep. 21 For since death came through a man, the resurrection of the dead comes also through a man. 22 For as in Adam all die, so in Christ all will be made alive. 23 But each in his own turn: Christ, the firstfruits; then, when he comes, those who belong to him.

When we think of Jesus' resurrection it should make us think of what he purchased – including our own resurrection. He is the first of the great harvest of the resurrection.

On that Day – Great Judgment

That day will also be a day of great judgment. Jesus will return in power, glory, and judgment that will make the entire earth quake. For unbelievers, that day will be the most terrible day they have ever experienced. God is patient and longsuffering towards those who have not repented in delaying that day. But it will come.

> **2 Peter 3:8-13**
>
> But do not forget this one thing, dear friends: With the Lord a day is like a thousand years, and a thousand years are like a day. 9 The Lord is not slow in keeping his promise, as some understand slowness. He is patient with you, not wanting anyone to perish, but everyone to come to repentance. 10 But the day of the Lord will come like a thief. The heavens will disappear with a roar; the elements will be destroyed by fire, and the earth and everything in it will be laid bare. 11 Since everything will be destroyed in this way, what kind of people ought you to be? You ought to live holy and godly lives 12 as you look forward to the day of God and speed its coming. That day will bring about the destruction of the heavens by

fire, and the elements will melt in the heat. 13 But in keeping with his promise we are looking forward to a new heaven and a new earth, the home of righteousness.

1 Corinthians 15:24

Then the end will come, when he hands over the kingdom to God the Father after he has destroyed all dominion, authority and power. 25 For he must reign until he has put all his enemies under his feet. 26 The last enemy to be destroyed is death.

This should terrify those who reject Christ. But, for Christians, it is a call to live holy lives, for we serve the living God.

On that Day - Final and Complete Judgment and the End of Death

That day will also be the end of death. Never again will physical death claim anyone. The fall will be reversed.

Revelation 20:11-15

Then I saw a great white throne and him who was seated on it. Earth and sky fled from his presence, and there was no place for them. 12 And I saw the dead, great and small, standing before the throne, and books were opened. Another book was opened, which is the book of life. The dead were judged according to what they had done as recorded in the books. 13 The sea gave up the dead that were in it, and death and Hades gave up the dead that were in them, and each person was judged according to what he had done. 14 Then death and Hades were thrown into the lake of fire. The lake of fire is the second death. 15 If anyone's name was not found written in the book of life, he was thrown into the lake of fire.

WSC 38. What benefits do believers receive from Christ at the resurrection?

At the resurrection, believers, raised in glory, will be publicly recognized and declared not guilty on the day of judgment and will be made completely happy in the full enjoyment of God forever.

The Christian will be declared "Not Guilty" on that day and made completely happy.

On that Day – Eternity Begins

So, consider that you will live forever. That can seem overwhelming and difficult to even begin to understand. Yet it is a glorious hope. The last chapter of the Bible begins with a description of the beginning of eternity.

> **Revelation 22:1-5**
>
> Then the angel showed me the river of the water of life, as clear as crystal, flowing from the throne of God and of the Lamb 2 down the middle of the great street of the city. On each side of the river stood the tree of life, bearing twelve crops of fruit, yielding its fruit every month. And the leaves of the tree are for the healing of the nations. 3 No longer will there be any curse. The throne of God and of the Lamb will be in the city, and his servants will serve him. 4 They will see his face, and his name will be on their foreheads. 5 There will be no more night. They will not need the light of a lamp or the light of the sun, for the Lord God will give them light. And they will reign forever and ever.

- God and Jesus are on the throne.
- Life is flowing as a river and a great harvest to God's people.
- All curse and suffering is past.
- We will see God's face and bear his name upon us!

- Night is over. We will bask in the glorious light of God forever.

- We will reign with Christ.

Review

Lesson 14 – We discussed our destiny. In other words – where are we going and where will we end up? If we know that our life will end well it brings great peace and confidence. Good news! God has an incredible destiny planned for his children - to be fully conformed to the likeness of Christ, to have the effects of the fall fully reversed, and to live in sinless joy. This will be glorious. In fact it is called glorification.

One day we will be glorified. That is, we will become perfect sons and daughters of God. We will be like Jesus in his character and live perfectly our purpose: to glorify God and enjoy him forever. When will this occur? After death we are immediately in the presence of God and our souls will be made perfect. At the return of Christ we will receive our resurrected bodies and then live forever with the Lord.

The second coming of Jesus will be the day of culmination. On that day:

- Everyone will be resurrected, believer and unbeliever.

- The dead in Christ will be raised like Jesus.

- God will judge every sin and reward his redeemed people.

- Death will be no more.

- Eternity will begin for all people. God's children will experience an eternity of life, worship, and reigning with Christ. Come Lord Jesus!

Prayer

- Father – your work for us is complete:
  - You have redeemed us
  - You have adopted us
  - You are sanctifying us
  - You will glorify us
  - We will follow you in resurrection
- You will come as the Glorious King:
  - Every tongue will confess you as King
  - You will judge every wrong
  - Death itself will be vanquished
  - Night will end. We will live in the light of your glory and reign with you
- We worship you, our God

Lesson 15

Joining the Visible Church

Professing our Faith and Joining with the People of God

Introduction

We have talked in recent lessons about our salvation – from effective calling to regeneration to faith to adoption to sanctification and in the last lesson glorification. But what do we do as Christians while here on earth?

The first lesson we talked about how God called a people to himself. These people are the Church – "the called out ones". The Church started with individuals, progressed to Abraham and his descendants - the people of Israel, and then to people from all the nations. To be a Christian is to part of God's Church.

The Church: Invisible and Visible

What is the invisible church?

It is the real church of Christ that we can't see. We are aware that we can never be completely sure who are true Christians.

WLC 64 What is the invisible church?

The invisible church is the whole number of the elect, that have been, are, or shall be gathered into one under Christ the Lord.

But does God know who are and will be his?

Yes. He knows who he has already redeemed and who he will redeem in the future.

Where then is the invisible church right now?

Those who have died are with Christ. Those still living are in the world.

One part of the invisible church is called the "church triumphant". What part is that?

Those Christians who are now with Christ in heaven are called the church triumphant.

What do you think the "church militant" is? Why?

The "church militant" is the invisible church on earth. It is called "militant" because all true Christians on earth struggle against sin and the devil.

What is the visible church?

The visible church is composed of all people who profess to be Christians, as well as their children.

Why do we call it the visible church?

Because we can see them gathered together into congregations and we hear them profess Christ.

Is it possible for someone to be a member of the visible church without being a member of the invisible church?

Yes. Sadly, someone can belong to a visible church and even claim to be a Christian and not be a true Christian.

Is it possible for someone to be a member of the invisible church while not a member of any part of the visible church?

Yes. However, it is abnormal and irregular. It is the duty of every Christian to unite with other Christians in some part of the visible church It is normal to be part of a local church.

When children of Christian parents who are part of the visible church are able, what is their duty?

> *Their duty is to make a public profession of faith and seek admission to the Lord's Table.*

The Church as a Family

How do we enter the family of God?

> *God adopts us.*

Who is the Father in the family?

> *God*

Who is your brother that was not adopted?

> *Jesus*

Who are your brothers and sisters in the family?

> *Other Christians*

What responsibilities do you have to God, your Father?

> *Obedience, love, honor, enjoyment, worship, allegiance, etc.*

What responsibilities do you have to your brothers and sisters?

> *Love, kindness, patience, honesty, care, instruction, correction, encouragement, etc...*

The Church as a Body

The Church is also described as being a body. Paul describes it in his letter to the Corinthians.

---

1 Corinthians 12:12-31

The body is a unit, though it is made up of many parts; and though all its parts are many, they form one body. So it is with Christ. 13 For we were all baptized by one Spirit into one body-whether Jews or Greeks, slave or free-and we were all given the one Spirit to drink.

14 Now the body is not made up of one part but of many. 15 If the foot should say, "Because I am not a hand, I do not belong to the body," it would not for that reason cease to be part of the body. 16 And if the ear should say, "Because I am not an eye, I do not belong to the body," it would not for that reason cease to be part of the body. 17 If the whole body were an eye, where would the sense of hearing be? If the whole body were an ear, where would the sense of smell be? 18 But in fact God has arranged the parts in the body, every one of them, just as he wanted them to be. 19 If they were all one part, where would the body be? 20 As it is, there are many parts, but one body.

21 The eye cannot say to the hand, "I don't need you!" And the head cannot say to the feet, "I don't need you!" 22 On the contrary, those parts of the body that seem to be weaker are indispensable, 23 and the parts that we think are less honorable we treat with special honor. And the parts that are unpresentable are treated with special modesty, 24 while our presentable parts need no special treatment. But God has combined the members of the body and has given greater honor to the parts that lacked it, 25 so that there should be no division in the body, but that its parts should have equal concern for each other. 26 If one part suffers, every part suffers with it; if one part is honored, every part rejoices with it.

27 Now you are the body of Christ, and each one of you is a part of it. 28 And in the church God has appointed first of all apostles, second prophets, third teachers, then workers of miracles, also those having gifts of healing, those able to help others, those with gifts of administration, and those speaking in different kinds of tongues. 29 Are all apostles? Are all

> prophets? Are all teachers? Do all work miracles? 30 Do all
> have gifts of healing? Do all speak in tongues? Do all
> interpret? 31 But eagerly desire the greater gifts.

Every Christian is a part of the Body of Christ.

But is everyone the same?

> *No. Just like the parts of a human body are different. The
> parts of the Church are different.*

What would happen if every part of your body were:

An eye? A foot? A nose? An ear?

So what point is Paul making?

> *Every Christian is part of the body and has a role in the
> body.*
>
> *We should all respect other Christians – we need them.*
>
> *We see Paul describe various roles in the Body of Christ –
> apostles, prophets, teachers, etc... Each person has a role
> and each of us is to care for and respect one another.*

We together as a Church are one in Christ. This should cause us
to love one another.

Paul talks about this in the next section of his letter – the
famous passage of 1 Corinthians 13; also called "The Love
Chapter". It describes the unity of the Body of Christ – the unity
of the Church.

---

1 Corinthians 12:31-13:7

And now I will show you the most excellent way.

13:1 If I speak in the tongues of men and of angels, but have
not love, I am only a resounding gong or a clanging cymbal. 2
If I have the gift of prophecy and can fathom all mysteries and
all knowledge, and if I have a faith that can move mountains,
but have not love, I am nothing. 3 If I give all I possess to the

poor and surrender my body to the flames, but have not love, I gain nothing.

4 Love is patient, love is kind. It does not envy, it does not boast, it is not proud. 5 It is not rude, it is not self-seeking, it is not easily angered, it keeps no record of wrongs. 6 Love does not delight in evil but rejoices with the truth. 7 It always protects, always trusts, always hopes, always perseveres.

Becoming a member of a visible church

A member is someone who has demonstrated a credible Christian confession and has connected to a local Christian church. A credible Christian confession is normally made before the leaders (elders) of the church and is often followed by a confession of faith before the members of the local church.

Many churches no longer have formal membership or membership vows. Why is membership important?

> *Membership enables accountability. In the New Testament Elders were appointed in every place to oversee the church and guide and protect it. This is God's design for the visible church. Consequently, it is an important duty for every Christian to be identified with a particular church, participate in its life, and be accountable to biblical church leadership. A Christian must be known by the elders for such accountability to take place. We will learn more of the role of the Elder in the next lesson.*

Examples from the Presbyterian Church in America

The Presbyterian Church of America (PCA) is a confessional denomination that holds to the reformed standards as expressed in the Westminster Confession of Faith and Catechisms. I have been part of the PCA and am using some of its documents as an example of becoming a member in a visible church.

The PCA has written standards of church governance that summarize the teaching of Scripture. The Book of Church

Order (BCO) of the PCA has three sections: the Form of
Government, the Rules of Discipline, and the Directory for
Worship.

The PCA BCO regarding the visible church:

2-1.   The Visible Church before the law, under the law, and
         now under the Gospel, is one and the same and consists
         of all those who make profession of their faith in the
         Lord Jesus Christ, together with their children.

The PCA BCO on joining a PCA visible church:

6-4.   Only those who have made a profession of faith in Christ,
have been baptized, and admitted by the Session to the Lord's
Table, are entitled to all the rights and privileges of the church.
(See *BCO* 57-4 and 58-4)

Here we see that to become a member of a church in the PCA
requires that your profession of faith be heard (it is examined),
that you have been baptized (either prior to your confession as a
child or after your profession of faith). You are then admitted
to the Lord's Table (communion) by the Elders of the church.

Understanding the fundamental Christian beliefs

Making a credible profession of faith requires a simple but clear
understanding of Christian fundamentals. These include who
God is, the nature and authority of scripture (specific
revelation), and the work of Christ in salvation. The following
is the PCA statement of belief:

We believe the Bible is the written word of God, inspired by
the Holy Spirit and without error in the original manuscripts.
The Bible is the revelation of God's truth and is infallible
and authoritative in all matters of faith and practice.

We believe in the Holy Trinity. There is one God, who exists
eternally in three persons: the Father, the Son, and the Holy
Spirit.

We believe that all are sinners and totally unable to save themselves from God's displeasure, except by his mercy.

We believe that <u>salvation is by God alone</u> as he sovereignly chooses those he will save. We believe his choice is based on his grace, not on any human individual merit, or foreseen faith.

We believe that Jesus Christ is the eternal Son of God, who through his perfect life and sacrificial death atoned for the sins of all who will trust in him, alone, for salvation.

We believe that God is gracious and faithful to his people not simply as individuals but as families in successive generations according to his covenant promises.

We believe that the Holy Spirit indwells God's people and gives them the strength and wisdom to trust Christ and follow him.

We believe that Jesus will return, bodily and visibly, to judge all mankind and to receive his people to himself.

We believe that all aspects of our lives are to be lived to the glory of God under the Lordship of Jesus Christ.

Making a Public Profession of Faith

The PCA BCO on making a public confession of faith:

BCO 57-5. (All of) you being here present to make a public profession of faith, are to assent to the following declarations and promises, by which you enter into a solemn covenant with God and his Church.

[These questions are asked as part of the public confession]

1. Do you acknowledge yourselves to be sinners in the sight of God, justly deserving his displeasure, and without hope save in his sovereign mercy?

Related Question: Why do you personally need salvation?

2. Do you believe in the Lord Jesus Christ as the Son of God, and Savior of sinners, and do you receive and rest upon him alone for salvation as He is offered in the Gospel?

Related Question: What is your hope for salvation?

Related Question: Tell us the story of your coming to faith in Christ as Savior.

Related Question: What is the basis of that hope?

Related Question: Who is Jesus Christ?

3. Do you now resolve and promise, in humble reliance upon the grace of the Holy Spirit, that you will endeavor to live as becomes the followers of Christ?

Related Question: What does it mean to be a follower of Christ? Why is being part of a church important to being that follower?

4. Do you promise to support the Church in its worship and work to the best of your ability?

Related Question: What is your role in supporting the Church in its worship and work?

Do you submit yourselves to the government and discipline of the Church, and promise to study its purity and peace?

Related Question: Do you submit to the government and discipline of the Church? What does it mean to study the purity and peace of the Church?

Review

Lesson 15 – There are two terms that are used to describe Christ's church. The first is the invisible church, which is the whole number of the elect who have been, are, or will be gathered into one under Christ. One part of the invisible church is the "church triumphant" – those who are now in heaven with Christ triumphantly. The other part of the invisible church is called the "church militant" – those Christians who are alive on earth and battle the world, the sin, and the devil.

Only God knows who are truly his. Because of this, we can only know the visible church that we see – those who have professed Christ as part of Christian congregations. Unfortunately, not all who profess Christ are truly born of the Spirit, so it is possible to be a member of the visible church and not part of the invisible church. Also it is possible to not be part of a visible congregation and yet be a true Christian, but this is not normal.

The church is a family with God as father, Christ as brother, and other Christians as siblings. Because we are part of God's family we should love and honor God and care for and love fellow Christians. The church is also a body. We each have a role in the healthy functioning of the body. We should be content and joyful in our place in the body while respecting the roles of our fellow Christians. We need one another.

Using the example from the Presbyterian Church in America we talked about how one becomes a communing member of a Church. This involves making a profession of faith, baptism, and taking vows before the congregation that affirm your hope in Christ and commitment to serve Christ in this fellowship.

Prayer

- Father – we thank you that by the work of Jesus we are your children, and part of your family, the Church
  - You have joined us to the church, the body of Christ
  - You call us to take our place in the visible church, the gathering of professing Christians
  - You call us to live and serve within your church
  - You call us to love one another and live with others in love, humility, service, and hope
  - You have called us to seek the peace and purity of your church
- Help us Father to live as obedient children and to honor and glorify you as we take our place of service within our church
- We pray for anyone who is not yet part of your invisible church and we pray that you would bring him or her to faith in the Savior and that they would then make a profession of faith and join a visible church

Lesson 16

How the Church Works

God's Design for the Visible Church

Introduction

So how does the church operate? Who are the leaders? Who makes decisions? Who does God appoint to watch over the Church and keep it on the right track?

There are various types of church governments. Some churches are congregational and are governed by the vote of the congregation. The pastor primarily governs some churches. A board governs some churches. Some churches are governed by a group of elders or deacons. In this lesson we examine the role of pastors, elders, and deacons.

Elders and Deacons

The apostle Paul describes how local churches were started and organized in the early Church.

Titus 1:1-9

Paul, a servant of God and an apostle of Jesus Christ for the faith of God's elect and the knowledge of the truth that leads to godliness- 2 a faith and knowledge resting on the hope of eternal life, which God, who does not lie, promised before the beginning of time, 3 and at his appointed season he brought his word to light through the preaching entrusted to me by the command of God our Savior,

4 To Titus, my true son in our common faith:

Grace and peace from God the Father and Christ Jesus our Savior.

5 The reason I left you in Crete was that you might straighten out what was left unfinished and appoint elders in every town, as I directed you. 6 An elder must be blameless, the husband of but one wife, a man whose children believe and are not open to the charge of being wild and disobedient. 7 Since an overseer is entrusted with God's work, he must be blameless-not overbearing, not quick-tempered, not given to drunkenness, not violent, not pursuing dishonest gain. 8 Rather he must be hospitable, one who loves what is good, who is self-controlled, upright, holy and disciplined. 9 He must hold firmly to the trustworthy message as it has been taught, so that he can encourage others by sound doctrine and refute those who oppose it.

Who was the Apostle that was sent out by Christ to the Gentiles?

Paul

Who did Paul send out to organize Churches?

Titus

What was Titus to do?

Appoint Elders (Presbyters) in each town (each congregation)

Presbyter is from the Greek work *presbuteros*, which means elder or senior. Those who are mature in the faith (and usually older in age) are appointed to church leadersip.

What is another name for an Elder?

An overseer (vs 7). This is the word, "Bishop".

Bishop is from the Greek word *episkopos*, which means superintendent or overseer. An Elder is an overseer of the local church.

What is the main responsibility of the elder?

To hold true to the gospel of Jesus, encourage Christians in right belief and living, and to resist and refute those who would hurt the peace and purity of the church.

What does Paul tell Titus that an Elder should be like?

A mature Christian man, blameless, has one wife, has Christian children, patient, self-controlled, holy, disciplined, hospitable, and faithful.

---

1 Timothy 3:1-13

Here is a trustworthy saying: If anyone sets his heart on being an overseer, he desires a noble task. 2 Now the overseer must be above reproach, the husband of but one wife, temperate, self-controlled, respectable, hospitable, able to teach, 3 not given to drunkenness, not violent but gentle, not quarrelsome, not a lover of money. 4 He must manage his own family well and see that his children obey him with proper respect. 5(If anyone does not know how to manage his own family, how can he take care of God's church?) 6 He must not be a recent convert, or he may become conceited and fall under the same judgment as the devil. 7 He must also have a good reputation with outsiders, so that he will not fall into disgrace and into the devil's trap.

8 Deacons, likewise, are to be men worthy of respect, sincere, not indulging in much wine, and not pursuing dishonest gain. 9 They must keep hold of the deep truths of the faith with a clear conscience. 10 They must first be tested; and then if there is nothing against them, let them serve as deacons.

11 In the same way, their wives are to be women worthy of respect, not malicious talkers but temperate and trustworthy in everything.

12 A deacon must be the husband of but one wife and must manage his children and his household well. 13 Those who have served well gain an excellent standing and great assurance in their faith in Christ Jesus.

What are some other traits of an Elder that Paul mentions?

Gentle, able to teach, not a lover of money, good with his family, not a new Christian, good reputation with non-Christians.

Besides Elders (overseers), what other officer does Paul refer to?

Deacons

What is the role of a Deacon?

Deacons serve the people of the church and the community. They help people with needs such as hunger, homelessness, sickness, etc...

Deacon is from the Greek word *diakonos*, which means a servant or waiter. Deacons in the church attend to the physical needs of the church members.

In these Scriptures Paul describes Elders and Deacons as men. What about women? Can they hold these offices?

This is an area of disagreement among Christians.

Some churches hold that these passages limit the offices to men only. They do so in reverence for Scripture and believe that these passages are prescriptive for the Church throughout history. It is a limitation in the office that God prescribes and not a matter of women being less valuable or capable than men.

Other churches have women as Elders and/or Deacons. They believe that other passages in the New Testament refer to women leaders in the church and this opens the office to both men and women. They would consider these passages as descriptive of specific churches situations and not a prescription for all churches.

What is a Presbyterian form of Government?

It means that elders lead the local church as taught in the New Testament (in the passages we have covered and others).

Is a Pastor the same thing as an Elder?

Some churches distinguish two types of Elders: Ruling Elders and Pastors (sometimes called Teaching Elders).

When two types of elders are recognized usually there is one elder in a church who is the Pastor. Larger churches sometimes have more than one Pastor or teaching elder, with one being distinguished as the Senior Pastor. Pastors usually have special training to preach and teach the Bible and often have the primary responsibility of preaching in the church.

Some churches only recognize one type of Elder, although there may be differences in responsibilities according to differences in abilities or training.

What is a Session?

In a Presbyterian church, when the Elders of a church meet together for the purpose of governing the church, they are called the Session. The term "Session" is from the language of a court: "The court is in session". In session the Elders together govern the church, pray for the church, and administer church discipline.

What is a Presbytery?

When the Elders from a group of churches in one area gather together it is called the Presbytery. The Presbytery meets to examine and affirm Elders, make decisions as a group of churches, and oversee issues that cannot be resolved by the Sessions of the churches.

What is a General Assembly?

When representatives from each presbytery meet together, this is called the General Assembly. The General Assembly meets to discuss issues that are important to all the churches in all the presbyteries.

<u>Review</u>

Lesson 16 – The New Testament teaches us about two offices that God has established to provide care and leadership for the local church. These offices are Elder and Deacon.

We learned about the office of Elder through two letters of Paul – one to Titus and another to Timothy. There we learn that an Elder (presbyter) is to be a mature Christian who can teach, and is well respected both inside and outside of the church. An elder is also called an overseer. Elders are charged with maintaining both right belief and right living within the church so as to honor and glorify God.

The second office of Deacon is described in both the letter to Timothy and in the book of Acts and several other references. Deacons are also officers of the local church and have the responsibility of seeing that practical care is given to those in need in the church and in the community. Deacons must also be mature and respectable, able to serve well.

We lastly learned about the levels of government within the Presbyterian form of government. Elders of a local church comprise a Session that oversees that church. Elders from among the churches in an area form the Presbytery. Presbyteries together form a general assembly.

Prayer

- Father – we thank you for making as a part of your church with the leaders you have appointed
    - We pray for each Elder and Deacon in our church
    - We pray that you would enable them to govern and serve well
    - We pray for all levels of church leadership that they would be used for the peace and purity of the church
    - We pray that our church would be faithful to your Scriptures, and that we as a family would honor and glorify you and be part of your work of calling people to yourself

Lesson 17

Living as a Christian

Part of the Body of Christ

Introduction

We have learned how important the Church is. It is God's own family and functions as a body – the body of Christ! The final lesson considers the diligent life of a Christian within the church where the people of God worship, pray, study, fellowship, and serve together.

Faith with Diligence

WSC 85. What does God require of us to escape his anger and the curse which we deserve?

To escape God's anger and curse, which we deserve for our sin, God requires from us faith in Jesus Christ and repentance unto life along with diligent involvement in all the external ways Christ uses to bring us the benefits of redemption.

The Christian life begins with the effectual call of God, resulting in our conversion.

In review, what are the two parts of conversion?

Faith and Repentance

Faith = turning to Jesus and his work

Repentance unto life = Turning from our sins

WSC 87. What is repentance unto life?

Repentance unto life is a saving grace, by which a sinner, being truly aware of his sinfulness. Understands the mercy of God in Christ, grieves for and hates his sins, and turns from them to God, fully intending and striving for a new obedience.

The key parts of repentance unto life:

- Realize our sinfulness

- Understand the Gospel

- Grieve for and hate our sins

- Turn from our sins to God

- Strive for a new obedience (live for God)

Means of Grace

How does God assist us in living for him?

- *The indwelling Holy Spirit who turns our heart to God*

- *Prayer to talk to and receive from God*

- *His Word (the Scriptures) to teach us*

- *Sacraments to feed our faith*

- *Worship of God*

- *A Christian family to love and serve with, that encourage us, teaches us, and corrects us*

- *Through acts of loving and sacrificial service*

These ways that God assists us in living for him are called the "Means of Grace", which is another way of saying what WSC 85 called "the external ways". The Means of Grace are gifts from God to us that enable our maturing in Christ.

Do you see how important it is to be part of the church? What would you miss if you were not part of a church?

- *Fellowship*

- *Preaching*

- *Corporate prayer*

- *The sacraments*

- *Service to the family*

Some Christians substitute quiet devotions for participation in the local church. What would be absent from your life if you lived this way?

- *Hearing the word preached with other Christians*

- *Praying with other Christians*

- *Worshipping with other Christians*

- *Receiving the sacraments*

- *Serving and encouraging other Christians*

- *Using the gifts God has given you within the family*

The danger of neglecting fellowship

The following story has been used to illustrate the danger of a Christian neglecting to join with other Christians in encouragement, service, and worship:

An Elder was with a Christian who had been absent from church for some time. They sat before a roaring fire and talked about various things happening in their lives for several hours. As the fire was burning down the elder asked, "We miss you at church. I was wondering what has prevented you from being with your church family. I would like to know what is happening with you. Could you tell me?" After some delay the answer came slowly and uncomfortably. He replied, "It is just that I feel more comfortable worshipping and praying alone. I think it is just better for me. I hope you can understand". Before answering the elder gazed into the dying flames. Without speaking he reached out and with the fire tongs moved one glowing coal away from the rest of the stack. Silence settled between the two for several minutes as both looked into the glowing coals. Slowly the one coal that was separated from the rest started to lose its glow… bright orange… red…dark red…grey… dark grey

What was the Elder illustrating with the coals?

When we remove ourselves from the church family, it impacts our Christian life. Our passion, witness, assurance, joy, and ministry are all hurt. Think of the Body of Christ. How well does a single part of the body do when separated from the whole body?

What do they do when someone has their finger cut off?

It is packed it in ice (to slow down the decay) until the surgeon can re-attach it to the body. We would never think that the finger could live by itself. There would be no blood flow to nourish and cleanse the finger. There would be nothing for the finger to do on its own even if it was healthy. We are the same – we need to be attached to the body of Christ to be healthy and productive.

The Sacraments

We have talked about all the external ways or means of grace that God provides to us within the church in order to grow and mature us. The sacraments are an important part of our growth.

The sacraments are an outward symbol of spiritual reality.

Jesus instituted the sacraments as a means of feeding and strengthening our faith. They remind us of the Covenant of Grace by representing it to us. They speak the gospel to us. They bring benefits of our redemption to us – God is actually present and brings growth and assurance through the sacraments.

What two sacraments did Jesus give us?

Baptism and the Lord's Supper

What does Baptism signify?

We are joined to Christ. Our sin has died with him, and we are cleansed (washed), and then raised with him to new life.

Who should be baptized?

New Christians and the infant children of believers should be baptized.

What does the Lord's Supper (Communion) signify?

Christ died for us and he is our hope of salvation and deliverance from God's judgment. We proclaim Christ as Savior until he comes again. We are now part of the body of Christ. We are united to Christ.

---

1 Corinthians 11:23-26

For I received from the Lord what I also passed on to you: The Lord Jesus, on the night he was betrayed, took bread, 24 and when he had given thanks, he broke it and said, "This is my body, which is for you; do this in remembrance of me." 25 In the same way, after supper he took the cup, saying, "This cup is the new covenant in my blood; do this, whenever you drink it, in remembrance of me." 26 For whenever you eat this bread and drink this cup, you proclaim the Lord's death until he comes.

1 Corinthians 10:16-17

Is not the cup of thanksgiving for which we give thanks a participation in the blood of Christ? And is not the bread that we break a participation in the body of Christ? 17 Because there is one loaf, we, who are many, are one body, for we all partake of the one loaf.

When we take communion we are participating in the broken body of our Savior. We are his and he is ours. Also – we partake together of one broken loaf. We are united together as family.

Revisiting the Questions of Church Membership

Do you confess Jesus as your savior and Lord – the only hope of salvation? Do desire to honor and glorify him all the days of your life and to worship and follow him always?

Do you acknowledge yourselves to be sinners in the sight of God, justly deserving his displeasure, and without hope save in his sovereign mercy?

Do you believe in the Lord Jesus Christ as the Son of God, and Savior of sinners, and do you receive and rest upon him alone for salvation as He is offered in the Gospel?

Do you now resolve and promise, in humble reliance upon the grace of the Holy Spirit, that you will endeavor to live as becomes the followers of Christ?

Do you promise to support the Church in its worship and work to the best of your ability?

Do you submit yourselves to the government and discipline of the Church, and promise to study its purity and peace?

Answer these questions for yourself. If you are able to say yes to these questions, find a church, make your profession of faith there and be joined to the visible community of faith. That Church will rejoice with you in your faith and conversion. They will pray for you often. They will love you well and help you to grow in your faith and service.

If you are not able to profess Christ, or have remaining questions regarding Christianity, I encourage you also to continue learning, find a church, and carefully examine the person and work of Jesus.

Back to the beginning

The first thing we talked about in the first lesson was: "What is the purpose of your life?" I leave you with the very first answer that was given in that first lesson. I hope you never forget the first catechism question or stop marveling at its truth and how deeply it can and should impact your life.

WSC 1. What is the Purpose of Man?

To Glorify God and Enjoy him forever

I hope and pray that you live your whole life according to this purpose. There is no higher purpose and there is no greater joy in the entire universe.

Soli Deo Gloria – To God Only Be The Glory

About the Author

William Frye is a brother, scientist, photographer, writer, businessman, church elder, and a passionate teacher.

Lesson Summaries

Lesson 1   Our purpose as People

We as people have a purpose from God: To glorify him and enjoy him forever. This purpose brings meaning and direction for all of our life.

Lesson 2   How God Can Be Known

We need to hear from God directly to live out our purpose. We learned that the voice of God that speaks in creation and our consciences is not enough due to our fallen condition. But God has spoken clearly to us! He has done so through the scriptures and his word teaches us what we must believe about God and what he requires of us.

Lesson 3   What is God Like?

We need to hear from God directly to live out our purpose. We learned that the voice of God that speaks in creation and our consciences is not enough due to our fallen condition. But God has spoken clearly to us! He has done so through the scriptures and his word teaches us what we must believe about God and what he requires of us.

Lesson 4   God the Three in One

God is one God who exists in three persons. Although truly one unity, there are tri (three persons) who are equally God in every respect of their being, wisdom, power, holiness, justice, goodness, and truth. Each person of the Trinity (tri-unity): Father, Son, and Holy Spirit are equally infinite, eternal, and unchangeable. Yet there is one God.

Lesson 5   God's Decrees

God is infinite in his knowledge, wisdom, and power. He is also unchangeable and eternal. Accordingly every intention and plan of God is final, eternal, and is realized perfectly. We call his plans decrees. God need not seek advice or counsel to form his decrees, as they are based upon his own good pleasure and are for his own glory. His decrees (plans) include every aspect of his creation and are worked out through his creation and providential care. Even the decisions and actions of men, freely chosen, are mysteriously but absolutely part of God's decrees. God's sovereign secret decrees are not revealed to men through revelation. We are to live our lives by obeying his revealed will, seeking God's glory, pursuing wisdom, and freely choosing our path as we glorify and enjoy God.

Lesson 6   Sin

God created Adam in his own image and in a state of total righteousness. Adam was given a will (the ability to make choices). God was clear in his instruction about the consequences of obedience (Eternal life) and disobedience (death). Adam fell because he did not glorify God through obedience. The results were guilt, lack, corruption, and death for Adam and all mankind. Because of Adam's fall, all mankind fell. This is called original sin.

Lesson 7   The Law of God

The Bible teaches what God requires of man. Every person must obey God's revealed will to attain eternal life. God reveals his nature and will in his natural creation and in his revelation to us through scripture. The moral law of God is summarized in the Ten Commandments. The Ten Commandments comprehensively summarize our duty to love God totally and our neighbor as we do ourselves.

Lesson 8   Jesus and the Covenant of Grace

The Covenant of Works was an arrangement made by God, which formed the basis of how mankind could gain eternal life by works of obedience to God. The Covenant of Works was the representative of mankind Adam. He was promised eternal life for himself and his descendants if he obeyed and death and alienation if he disobeyed. The Covenant of Works is also called the Covenant of Life.

The Covenant of Grace was made in eternity past between God and his son Jesus. The Covenant of Grace established that righteousness and salvation was only obtained through the work of the seed of the woman – Christ the second Adam. Immediately after the fall it was revealed in that the descendent of Eve would conquer Satan and death and would be wounded in doing so.

Christ our Redeemer purchases his people by paying the purchase price (ransom) of perfect obedience to God's moral law and by baring the penalty of our sin for us, which is death. This is a free gift. We are saved by grace alone by faith alone because of Christ alone.

Lesson 9   Jesus – His Person and Work

We learned from WSC 21 that: There is only one redeemer for mankind – Jesus Christ, the eternal Son of God. God chooses those who are redeemed. God the Son became a man – though he was not always a man. Jesus continues to be both man and God to this day and will remain so forever. Jesus has two natures – God and man, yet he is one person.

The names of Jesus tell us much about him: Immanuel (God with us), Jesus (Jehovah saves), Christ (Messiah or Anointed One). There are many other names and titles of Christ throughout the Scriptures. Jesus has two natures: human and divine. Only a man could pay the debt of obedience to the moral law that was owed by man. Only a perfect man without debt to

God could pay the ransom. Only God and not a man alone could have sufficient value to redeem the multitude of God's elect.

The resurrection of Christ is the central event in Christianity. It demonstrated that Jesus is the Son of God; he fully satisfied God's wrath due to the sins of the people; he conquered death; he conquered Satan; he is the lord of the living and the dead.

Finally, we learned that Jesus is our prophet, priest, and king. As prophet he reveals the will of God and way of salvation. As priest he offers himself up once to satisfy divine justice and to reconcile us to God. As king he brings us under his power, rules and defends us, and conquers all his and our enemies.

Lesson 10   Jesus – Justification and Adoption

God's response to sin is to impose a penalty – alienation and death. God cannot merely pardon sin without a payment, for this would deny his holiness and justice. Also, if God merely pardoned sin – we would not be secure in our pardon, as God could deny himself again by reversing his pardon and punishing us.

We examined the Jewish tabernacle and how sacrifices were made in ancient Israel to address the sins of the people. Once a year, on the Day of Atonement, the High Priest would make a sacrifice for all the people in the Most Holy Place. The book of Hebrews describes how all this pointed to the work of our great High Priest – Jesus. Jesus entered the Holy Place in Heaven once to present himself as the sacrifice for his people. This has brought permanent forgiveness, access to God, and a clear conscience.

We studied justification; which is being declared righteous based upon the work of Christ. But, we are not only justified, but adopted! We are made children of the living God and given the Holy Spirit by which we cry "Abba Father", knowing that we love God, are accepted by him, and will dwell with him forever.

Lesson 11   The Holy Spirit and Effectual Calling

First we learned about the Holy Spirit and his role by walking through the gospel of John. We learned that: the Holy Spirit:

- Anointed Jesus for his ministry
- Convicts men of sin and points to Christ as Savior
- Gives spiritual birth to men
- Indwells God's people and guides them in true worship
- Is our Comforter and Counselor and Teacher

One of the most important things the Holy Spirit does is to cause those who are dead in sins to be saved. The truth is that we are dead spiritually and unable to come to faith without the Holy Spirit changing our heart. We take part in the redemption Christ bought when the Holy Spirit effectively applies it to us. The Spirit applies to us the redemption Christ bought by producing faith in us and so uniting us to Christ in our effective calling. Why are we saved? Because the Holy Spirit effectively applies the work of Christ to us.

Where did your faith come from? This is the bottom line: we would no more come to faith without the miracle work of the Holy Spirit than a dead man could climb out of his casket. Faith is given to us. It is not what we give to God. The result of effective calling is Salvation: The Holy Spirit convinces us that we are sinful and miserable. He enlightens our minds that Christ is Lord and Savior, and he transforms our hearts to embrace Christ.

Lesson 12   The Holy Spirit – Regeneration and Conversion

We studied the work of the Holy Spirit in our regeneration. Regeneration means to give life again. Regeneration is what the Holy Spirit does in us and for us at our conversion – he persuades us and makes us able to receive Jesus Christ. It took heart surgery to remove our heart of stone, enable us to place our trust in Christ, and give us spiritual life. We see this in John 3 with the story of Nicodemus. Nicodemus, a Pharisee was seeking wisdom for living that would enable him to better please God. Jesus tells Nicodemus that the secret to entering the kingdom of God was to be born again of the Spirit. This birth is not because of who we are or what we decide, but by the work of God that no one can predict.

We talked about Christian conversion. This is not deciding to be a Christian or to join a church. Again, it is the work of God in our life where we turn from our sin and put our faith in Christ and his work. Faith is the gift of God where we receive and rest on Christ alone for salvation, as he is freely offered to us in the gospel. As we turn to Christ we also turn from sin, hating it and intending and striving for a new obedience.

These steps in conversion are a result of the Holy Spirit working through the presented gospel:

- A sinner becomes truly aware of his sinfulness and,
- Understands the mercy of God in Christ and,
- Grieves for and hates his sin and,
- Turns from his sin to faith in Christ – fully intending and striving for new obedience.

Lesson 13   The Holy Spirit – Sanctification and Assurance

We discussed the three benefits that in this life result from our being effectively called by God: Justification, Adoption, and Sanctification. The first two are acts of God, which happen immediately at the time of our conversion. Sanctification, on the other hand, is a work of God that occurs over our lifetime and is not completed until the moment of our death.

Baptism shows us clearly that we both died and arose in Christ. We died to sin and its ways and arose with our Lord to a new life of righteousness as God's child. Hence, it is ridiculous for a Christian to continue to sin as a way of life. We are clearly commanded in Scripture to work hard before God, to please and honor him. We are to put off the old ways of death and estrangement and put on the new ways of righteousness and life. This includes the use of our tongue, all of our talents, our time, and our passions.

The benefits that come from our justification, adoption, and sanctification include our assurance of God's love, a peace of conscience, joy in the Holy Spirit, and growing and persevering in grace. Assurance comes from: proclaiming the gospel as true, by the presence of the Holy Spirit, obedience, fellowship, service, and all the means of grace.

If we lack repentance this leads to lost assurance, a lack of joy, and a lack of persevering in grace. If we find ourselves in this state, we are called to repent to the God who promises to restore us.

Lesson 14   The Future

We discussed our destiny. In other words – where are we going and where will we end up? If we know that our life will end well it brings great peace and confidence. Good news! God has an incredible destiny planned for his children - to be fully conformed to the likeness of Christ, to have the effects of the fall fully reversed, and to live in sinless joy. This will be glorious. In fact it is called glorification.

One day we will be glorified. That is, we will become perfect sons and daughters of God. We will be like Jesus in his character and live perfectly our purpose: to glorify God and enjoy him forever. When will this occur? After death we are immediately in the presence of God and our souls will be made perfect. At the return of Christ we will receive our resurrected bodies and then live forever with the Lord.

The second coming of Jesus will be the day of culmination. On that day:

- Everyone will be resurrected, believer and unbeliever.

- The dead in Christ will be raised like Jesus.

- God will judge every sin and reward his redeemed people.

- Death will be no more.

- Eternity will begin for all people. God's children will experience an eternity of life, worship, and reigning with Christ. Come Lord Jesus!

Lesson 15   Joining the Visible Church

There are two terms that are used to describe Christ's church. The first is the invisible church, which is the whole number of the elect who have been, are, or will be gathered into one under Christ. One part of the invisible church is the "church triumphant" – those who are now in heaven with Christ triumphantly. The other part of the invisible church is called the "church militant" – those Christians who are alive on earth and battle the world, the sin, and the devil.

Only God knows who are truly his. Because of this, we can only know the visible church that we see – those who have professed Christ as part of Christian congregations. Unfortunately, not all who profess Christ are truly born of the Spirit, so it is possible to be a member of the visible church and not part of the invisible church. Also it is possible to not be part of a visible congregation and yet be a true Christian, but this is not normal.

The church is a family with God as father, Christ as brother, and other Christians as siblings. Because we are part of God's family we should love and honor God and care for and love fellow Christians. The church is also a body. We each have a role in the healthy functioning of the body. We should be content and joyful in our place in the body while respecting the roles of our fellow Christians. We need one another.

Using the example from the Presbyterian Church in America we talked about how one becomes a communing member of a Church. This involves making a profession of faith, baptism, and taking vows before the congregation that affirm your hope in Christ and commitment to serve Christ in this fellowship.

Lesson 16   How the Church Works

The New Testament teaches us about two offices that God has established to provide care and leadership for the local church. These offices are Elder and Deacon.

We learned about the office of Elder through two letters of Paul – one to Titus and another to Timothy. There we learn that an Elder (presbyter) is to be a mature Christian who can teach, and is well respected both inside and outside of the church. An elder is also called an overseer. Elders are charged with maintaining both right belief and right living within the church so as to honor and glorify God.

The second office of Deacon is described in both the letter to Timothy and in the book of Acts and several other references. Deacons are also officers of the local church and have the responsibility of seeing that practical care is given to those in need in the church and in the community. Deacons must also be mature and respectable, able to serve well.

We lastly learned about the levels of government within the Presbyterian form of government. Elders of a local church comprise a Session that oversees that church. Elders from among the churches in an area form the Presbytery. Presbyteries together form a general assembly.

Lesson 17   Living as a Christian

God provides Means of Grace to assist us in living for him:

- The indwelling Holy Spirit who turns our heart to God
- Prayer to talk to and receive from God
- His Word (the Scriptures) to teach us
- Sacraments to feed our faith
- Worship of God
- A Christian family to love and serve with, that encourage us, teaches us, and corrects us
- Through acts of loving and sacrificial service

Made in the USA
San Bernardino, CA
07 September 2015